ADVANCE PRAISE FOR

THE DAY AFTER THE DAY AFTER

"*The Day After The Day* After is a stone-cold miracle: a riveting memoir, a shrewd examination of Hollywood flimflammery, a subversive history of Kansas, and a restless meditation on the American lust for violence and redemption. It is not only brilliantly structured, but compulsively honest and gorgeously written. I have no idea how the fuck Steven Church did all this, but I'd very much like to marry him. Or at least sleep with his heart."—STEVE ALMOND, author of *Not That You Asked, The Evil B.B. Chow*, and *Candyfreak*

"Steven Church has written a personal and haunting memoir that strings up history on a hangman's rope. Fear, belief, and hope struggle under the weight of popular culture. *The Day After The Day After* reveals how susceptible we all are when we're looking for meaning, and how easily we can be flattened by what we find. A beautiful, sadly funny, moving book." —ADAM BRAVER, author of *November 22, 1963* and *Mr. Lincoln's Wars*

"*The Day After The Day After* is like some kind of literary atom smasher, an irradiated Wikipedia Monster come to life. There is *so much* in this book but none of it is anything less than harrowing, funny, smart, and brutally insightful. I have never read a book that better captures what growing up in the Age of Reagan really felt like, and I suspect I never will." —TOM BISSELL, author of *The Father of All Things* and *Chasing the Sea*

"Steven Church's *The Day After The Day After* is an astonishing tour-de-force of story, vignette, and searing family drama that strikes at the heart of post-Cold War America. Brilliant, heartfelt, and surprising at every turn, Church's voice remains sane and insightful even as it reveals an apocalyptic world of people whose lives are shadowed by the threat of nuclear disaster, both real and imagined." —KRISTEN IVERSEN, author of *Molly Brown: Unraveling the Myth*

"*The Day After The Day After* is filled with catastrophes large and small, epic and personal, imagined and real. It is a bittersweet look back at a time in our nation's history when the fear of annihilation, of crimson mushroom clouds and nuclear winters, saturated our lives and altered the consciousness of our generation. It is Steven Church's wisdom and grace, his heartfelt and sincere storytelling, which saves us from destruction, allowing us to see another day through with gratitude and humility." —ALEX ESPINOZA, author of *Still Water Saints*

"A frightening and touching portrait of remarkable—and oddly inevitable—coincidences." —JOHN D'AGATA, author of *Halls of Fame*

THE DAY AFTER

My Atomic Angst

STEVEN CHURCH

Soft Skull Press

New York

For Rachel

Library of Congress Cataloging-in-Publication Data
Church, Steven.
The day after The day after : my atomic angst / Steven Church.
   p. cm.
Includes bibliographical references and index.
ISBN 978-1-59376-261-2 (alk. paper)
1. Church, Steven. 2. Church, Steven—Childhood and youth. 3. Cold War—Social aspects—United States. 4. Nuclear warfare—Social aspects—United States. 5. Day after (Motion picture) 6. Motion pictures—Influence—Case studies. 7. Motion picture locations—Kansas—Lawrence—History—20th century. 8. Lawrence (Kan.)—Biography. 9. Lawrence (Kan.)—Social life and customs—20th century. 10. United States—Social life and customs—1971– I. Title.
CT275.C5795A3 2010
978.1'65033092—dc22
[B]
                              2009041151

ISBN: 13: 978-1-59376-261-2

Cover design by Alvaro Villaneuva
Interior design by Elyse Strongin: Neuwirth & Associates, Inc.

Printed in the United States of America

Soft Skull Press
New York, NY

www.softskull.com

Contents

BOOK 1 IN THE BEGINNING

Tragic Prelude, by John Steuart Curry

Nuclear war is horrible and survival in its wake is abhorrent, even unimaginable, to civilized humanity.

—Rolling text at the end of *The Day After*

A History of Storms

IN THE EARLY morning on Friday, August 21, 1863, in Lawrence, Kansas, the air feels heavy and wet, as if the town were trapped in a steam press. It can often feel dank, humid, and stuffy, even at such an early hour. But morning is the best time. After that, the pressure just builds and pushes until the day cracks and splits open like a blister in the heat.

Downtown, at the southern end of Massachusetts Street, beneath the bridge, the wide and muddy Kansas River slams up against the Bowersock Mill's wooden dam. In the summer, when the banks are swollen, brown water rolls over the batter boards in a great beige wave.

Locals call it the Kaw and tell stories of boats trapped in the eddy currents, sucked back into the pour-over beneath the dam, smashed to bits and churned into mulch, the poor fishermen tangled up with the driftwood at the bottom where the giant catfish feed.

On this Friday morning in Kansas, as free men and women wake for a day of work in town or on nearby farms, other men and women, runaway slaves, retreat into underground rooms, caves, and bunkers. Many people in Lawrence have built safe houses and tunnels to neighboring homes, secret chambers behind fake walls, and other places to hide.

I IMAGINE A man who knows all this about his town. He sits on his porch that morning, trying to enjoy the sunrise—those soft penumbral hours before the day begins bright and busy and hot. He's a young man, in his late thirties, strapping and ruggedly handsome with a misshapen nose and large droopy ears. He has a beautiful wife who loves him unconditionally and two rambunctious boys. A practical man: He wears suspenders instead of a belt because they hold his pants up better. But he is also obsessive and eternally worried, the kind of person who feels the danger of the time pressing against his skull like someone is trying to shove his eyeball out from behind.

He may see or know more than he can articulate about what it means to live in a place known as "Bleeding Kansas." There's simply too much on his mind these days, too much at stake. The previous night, as he crawled into bed, his wife asked him if he felt bothered, but he couldn't find the words to articulate all that he felt.

He sips coffee and reads a book and scans the horizon. Maybe he's overreacting, paying too much attention to nagging instincts. But it's these moments of the day when he thinks most clearly. He wants to linger in these moments for a little longer.

IN THE DISTANCE, he hears the clatter of hooves and wagon wheels on the brick-paved streets. Because he does not know for sure what is coming, he feels no real fear. Not yet. He tries not to make too much of the noise. But he can't ignore the sounds, can't pretend that he doesn't hear the pepper of gunshots in the distance; perhaps, just as the sun bursts up over the horizon, he begins to recognize the way the noise doesn't fit into his dependable picture of the morning. Neighbors have left windows open, hoping for some relief. White curtains billow out in the infrequent breeze—tongues licking at the languid air—and Daniel wonders if anyone else hears what he hears.

He knows there have been many skirmishes lately, but steps have been taken to ensure the town's security. Guards have been posted, U.S. cavalry assigned to the town's perimeter. Assurances have been made and the people feel comfortable enough to relax a bit and loosen their vigilance. Lawrence no longer believes it is a target of attacks. The town's guns are—in a move that bothers Daniel, even if he does agree with it in principle—stored in a central armory, leaving most of the citizens unarmed.

The crickets are still singing, the cicadas buzzing and chittering in the grass. The sun casts a thin band of bright light, cutting first across the top of Mount Oread and then moving down into the shaded streets. Everything seems peaceful still.

Yet it has already begun.

ON THE MORNING of August 21, 1863, the pale, mustachioed twenty-five-year-old horse thief and cattle rustler William Quantrill led a gang of nearly 400 men and boys, most of them poor, illiterate farmers from Missouri, on a murderous rampage through the streets of Lawrence.

The attack happened quickly, with no warning and little mercy. Quantrill's raiders met, overwhelmed, and annihilated a small regiment of U.S. cavalry posted to protect the town, killing close to two dozen young, untrained soldiers. They then spread out into smaller roving bands. With weapons drawn and torches in hand, they systematically worked their way through the residential neighborhoods, screaming like banshees and firing their weapons to draw people from their beds.

Defenseless men and boys were shot on sight, point-blank or in the back, many still wearing their nightclothes, their bodies left where they fell in their yards. Entire blocks of homes and businesses were torched to the ground. The downtown was left in smoking ruins and much of the town's relative wealth was plundered and looted.

Survivors described the arrival of Quantrill's raiders like a sudden storm, but the clouds had been building on the horizon for some time, the tension boiling for years. It was inevitable that something would happen. Though most people don't realize it today, Kansas was a flash point for conflicts at the heart of the Civil War. Seven years earlier, in 1856, people had already witnessed the Sacking of Lawrence, yet another violent raid by a notorious Missouri bushwhacker, along with retaliation strikes on Missouri towns just over the border and other bloody skirmishes.

In the years before the war, the radical abolitionist John Brown and his brother Owen prowled around Kansas, hoping to incite a religious war, hacking pro-slavers to death with broadswords and shepherding runaways to safe houses in Lawrence and elsewhere.

The Kansas–Missouri border was perhaps just as divisive as the Mason–Dixon Line, with fervent abolitionists on one side and defiant slaveholders on the other. Quantrill's raid was the last and most devastating wound in the story of a place that came to be known as "Bleeding Kansas" and "Bloody Kansas."

During battles in the summer of 1863, the Confederacy seemed to be weakening significantly. It suffered crippling defeats at both Vicksburg and Gettysburg, and Lincoln signed his Emancipation Proclamation on January 1 of the same year. As a kid, I was always told that Kansas was the first state to support Lincoln's proclamation, and that our neighbor, Missouri—just 50 miles east of Lawrence—was the last state to sign the document, holding out until the end.

William Quantrill made his mark with pro-slavery sympathizers by stealing runaway slaves and returning them to their "owners" in Missouri, collecting handsome bounties in the process.

A charismatic but devious leader, he is repeatedly called a "guerrilla" fighter and "terrorist" in historical reports of the time, and by most accounts he held a personal grudge against several prominent Lawrence residents—most likely abolitionists or religious and community leaders, and one particular Jayhawker, Senator Lane, who was rumored to have escaped the carnage by fleeing into a cornfield in his nightshirt.

It was reported that some of Quantrill's own men paled at the horror that unfolded that morning and recoiled from the carnage. But not William Quantrill. He was undeterred and unaffected, and by most accounts relished the slaughter.

A WITNESS AND survivor to the massacre, the Reverend H.D. Fisher, would recall, "Such scenes of barbarity have never been witnessed, even in the days of war, in recent centuries, except among the most degraded tribes of earth."

Clearly deeply affected by what he witnessed, Fisher would continue, "Two-thirds of the people [of Lawrence] were homeless . . . That night, nearly an hundred widows and two hundred fatherless children sat wailing in the streets . . . Shorn of her pride and beauty and sons the city wept in sack-cloth and sat in ashes."

Whatever his motivations, whatever the cause, the effect of Quantrill's raid was that when they rode out of Lawrence four hours later, he and his men had killed between 150 and 200 people.

I IMAGINE ONE boy living through the slaughter, the youngest son of our lone sentinel on his porch. His father's namesake, Daniel Jr. emerges from the cellar unharmed and finds his father at the bottom of the front steps, his skull cleaved open, the gray mass of his brain exposed, and so much blood staining the bricks, coloring them an even deeper red, almost black. Something hardens in him at that moment, with that image of his father's dead eyes wide open. Something becomes cemented in his constitution, something beyond conviction or memory—something deeper, genetic, and elemental. A post-apocalyptic oracle is born that morning of Quantrill's raid in Lawrence, Kansas, and he provides the right eyes to see this story again from a different distance.

Born into the End

IT'S POSSIBLE THAT the apocalypse has always lurked in my blood, that I was born into it and destined to live in a world teetering on the edge of collapse—or at least one that felt that way.

My entire generation was, after all, conceived amid a collective angst, the news and noise of explosions, shootings, and riots that defined life in America during the late 1960s and early '70s—some of them a bit too close to home.

I was conceived during a time known in my hometown's history as the Days of Rage, a time when violence again surfaced in the streets of Lawrence.

The most newsworthy event—the sort of thing that's captured in film, archived, and relived—occurred just before 11:00 pm on April 20, 1970, when a loud blast pierced the air around the University of Kansas campus, not far from my parents' home. Employees of the Kansas Memorial Union felt the concussion, heard the alarms, and rushed upstairs to find a fire spreading quickly up the walls and out onto the roof, licking 30 to 40 feet into the air, painting the night sky in swaths of orange as thick black clouds billowed out over the town.

Part of the building's roof collapsed. Severe damage was done, but fortunately nobody was injured. The firebombing of the union—blamed by some on the underground dissident group the Weathermen and by others on local members of the Students for a Democratic Society—occurred during a week of riots, shootings, fires, antiwar protests, and other violent confrontations.

There were other less sensational events too—the kinds of things that have always lingered in the "unsolved mysteries" portion of my consciousness, that place in my brain that acts like a bird's gizzard, storing up food for thought, milling it with stones, processing it into something I can swallow.

My dad worked at the time for the largest real estate and property management firm in town, McGrew Real Estate. He was basically a low-level property manager. But it was a good job, his first real job out of college. He was just trying to work his way up in the company, so he did what was asked. He collected rent. He responded to calls at all hours regarding problems with properties around town—one of them a house rumored to be the local headquarters of the SDS.

He told me that most of the calls about that particular house came from an octogenarian across the street. She mostly complained of nudity and "fornication in the front yard," with the only serious call involving a stoned idiot who threw gasoline into a fireplace and nearly burned the house down.

Perhaps when the phone rang around three o'clock one morning during the Days of Rage, my dad was thinking it might be the hippies in the SDS house again, or maybe it was about some other problem with a rental property. He probably wasn't expecting to hear what he did.

The person on the phone, a police officer, asked, "Are you Ed Church? Do you work for McGrew Real Estate?"

When Dad confirmed this, the officer informed him that just an hour or so earlier, someone had heaved a pipe bomb through his office window. The bomb rolled right under Dad's desk.

I like to imagine that it lingered and hissed, sputtering and burning first—the cartoon sound of warning, the signal of one last chance—before it burst. I like to imagine that my father would have had time to get out if he happened to have been sitting there, working late as he often did, maybe just getting ready to return home to my mom. I like to think they weren't targeting him but something he represented—and Dad told me they probably *were* targeting McGrew just because of the company's stature in town. They'd also bombed the Capitol Federal Savings Building downtown. He told me he thought someone was just trying to "stick it to 'the Man,'" and my dad just happened to work for "the Man."

He also told me that when the pipe bomb exploded, it blew his chair up through the ceiling above and reduced his wooden desk to splinters and bits of paper.

It was during these days—though it's difficult to be sure precisely when—that a kind of martial law was imposed in Lawrence. National Guard troops were posted around town, a curfew was strictly enforced, and travel was restricted.

My dad remembered that he and my mother had to get a special pass to travel to Topeka to visit my grandparents, who were there for a conference of some kind. When they returned home, they had to show the pass at the turnpike entrance and travel down Iowa Street before turning east on 9th Street.

Dad said there were military vehicles everywhere, and standing in the intersection was a "snot-nosed kid" with an automatic weapon trained on them. As they turned and passed through the intersection, the kid and his gun stood a little over an arm's length away from my mom, just beyond the windshield glass. He pointed his rifle at my parents' car as they passed, the long, black muzzle tracking them through the turn.

TEN DAYS AFTER the firebombing of the Kansas Memorial Union, on April 30, Richard Nixon announced the U.S. invasion of Cambodia. At Kent State University in Ohio, students protested against these actions, and, much as it was in Lawrence, the National Guard was called in to help restore order. On May 4, 1970, the untrained young guardsmen from Ohio encountered a group of angry protesters on campus. Something happened. A spark. A word. A gesture. A wrong turn. And the guardsmen opened fire. When they stopped shooting, they'd killed four students and wounded nine others.

Dad told me that during this time he was living scared. He was afraid of the National Guard, afraid for his own safety, but he wasn't sure if that was before or after the bombings and the riots, before or after I was conceived.

He said the timeline is muddled up for him. Everything happened simultaneously in his memory. Kent State. The Days of Rage. My conception. He told me he has mostly impressions of that time— the spectral auras of memory. Things like facts and dates are elusive. But he has always recounted, during my entire childhood, the story about the National Guardsman posted on the corner of 9th and Iowa Streets, and I will admit that to this day, when I pass that corner, I see the guardsman too. Green fatigues. Helmet shading his eyes. Two shaky arms leveling the rifle at my mother's window.

"That was very frightening," Dad said. "I've never been so happy to get home."

My mom had begun to wonder if she would ever get pregnant,

began to wonder if it was her problem or if something was wrong with my dad, or if the universe or God or somebody was trying to tell them something, trying to say, "Are you crazy? Having a child in this world?"

I have counted back and it would be about right. I was made amid the rage. Mom had almost given up hope by the time the National Guard rolled into town and restored order in Lawrence, setting up camp on street corners and patrolling campus.

Most likely I was a tiny mass of cells, perhaps a fluttering heartbeat, as the violence descended like a cloud. I was little more than blood and muscle when I first felt the creeping end—but I was also a statement of hope, a promise for my parents.

My son existed as the same mass of cells and kinetic possibility when the events of 9/11 changed the American understanding of apocalypse. Like me, he was born into wars both tangible and abstract—Vietnam and the Cold War for me, Iraq and the War on Terror for him. I hope he's lucky enough to know his wars from a distance and mainly through books, movies, and TV shows, but I wonder what those media windows will be for him and how they have already been opened by my generation.

He was only six when, in a recent local mayoral election in Fresno, California, he became preoccupied with a proposal to build a nuclear power plant in town, not far from our home.

"Daddy," he asked me one day as we were driving, "why would someone want to build a nuclear power plant here?"

"I don't know," I said. "It would probably bring a lot of jobs to the area. And some people support it now as a better alternative to oil."

"But it will kill us all," he said.

"Who told you that?"

"Mommy."

"Really?"

"Uh-huh. She said that it would melt and everybody in Fresno would die."

"No," I said. "She's talking about a meltdown, an accident. Those hardly ever happen." I didn't mention anything about Three Mile Island or Chernobyl. "And even if there was an accident, it wouldn't necessarily kill us all."

"She said it would kill us later too, with cancer. Like Aunt Belle and Grandfather."

"Yeah," I paused. I didn't know what to say. We've never been the kind of parents who shield him from the truth. "She may be right about that. Nuclear waste is bad stuff."

I thought about my own fears of a nuclear accident and the Wolf Creek nuclear power plant, just seventy-five miles from where I grew up. I thought about how my parents tried to reassure me after Three Mile Island. On some level I understood what he felt. We were all going to die. But I also understood that his idea of the apocalypse would be both strikingly similar and markedly different from my own. I had no idea how to explain any of this to him.

I tried anyway, because I am a father and that's my job. I'm supposed to give him hope. "Don't worry. They'll never get the money to build that thing. It's not going to happen," I said.

"Really?" He stared at me through the rear-view mirror.

"Sure," I said. "Besides, if it does, we'll move."

He smiled. "We'll move?"

"You bet," I said, and I told him that we wouldn't live near a nuclear power plant, that we'd move somewhere safe. I tried to give him the hope of escape. It wasn't much, but it was something. I didn't tell him that I had no idea to where we would escape.

I didn't tell him that he had been born on the Front Range of Colorado, neighbor to Minuteman silos, military bases, oil refineries, the old Rocky Flats plutonium pit facility, and the secluded NORAD complex hidden away in the mountains somewhere above Colorado Springs. We couldn't escape back to his place of birth, to the first place he knew as home.

I didn't mention that he was a fluttering heartbeat, a mass of impressionable cells, when 9/11 happened, or that we had spent a month in the summer of 2007 in a Madrid hotel just a block away from the subway line bombed by terrorists in 2004.

We don't necessarily shield him from the truth, but we also don't always point out just how fragile his life might be or just how close we've taken him to the edge. I figure there will be plenty of other texts to tell him this, plenty of reminders that we're all sliding toward total immolation.

Early Visions

LIKE MOST CHILDREN growing up in '70s and '80s America, I imagined we'd all be dead in ten years. But my belief was based on more than the facts of nuclear proliferation. Before I hit kindergarten, I'd seen the end coming. I'd seen our future and it wasn't pretty.

The visions generally began the same for me. Awake in my bed, covers pulled up to my chin, teeth rattling in my skull from a high fever, I'd try in vain to sleep. My head clogged full of phlegm and ineffective drugs, I'd watch the numbers on my alarm clock spin like pinwheels, the minutes ticking off in seconds. I closed my eyes and opened them again, closed them and opened them—deliberately trying to slow the pulsing. The light from the hall seemed to flicker and pop and surge under the door.

Then the images came and transported me to another world, another time. I saw what appeared to be a scale model of our neighborhood built from balsa wood and matchsticks. I hovered over the houses, stared down from above, and realized it wasn't a model at all. It was real and there were tiny people in the tiny town—my family, friends, and neighbors—little ant-sized humans scurrying around the village. I recognized their miniature features, their hats and coats, their tiny briefcases and umbrellas. I heard something, or felt a presence, and looked over my shoulder.

For reasons or causes that were never entirely clear, a torrent of water rushed toward the neighborhood. I saw it coming down the valley where our neighborhood, Alvamar, was located. It roiled and churned up rocks and trees until it became a wall of water and debris. This made no sense to me. There was no logic, no rational explanation for the coming flood.

It was just there—the end of the world.

I tried to warn everyone—my mother, my father, my brother—tried to make them understand, but they couldn't hear me, and I watched helplessly as the flood swept into town, flattened the match-stick homes and scoured all the life away, leaving a path of rubble and limbs and bones. My neighborhood sat in sack-cloth and ashes.

Everything I knew was destroyed.

Or at least it was in my imagination.

The doctors called them "febrile seizures," and told my parents that I may have suffered brain damage from my fevers. They said I could be at risk for epilepsy later in life. My parents did everything they could to stop the fevers. They took me to all the doctors, and I ingested a steady regimen of antibiotics for most of my kindergarten year in school—something we wouldn't dream of doing now with the increased fear of antibiotic overload. Sometimes I blacked out from my fevers and woke up in my father's arms, the two of us standing in a cold shower. Sometimes the drugs kept the hallucinations away. But the images remained in my head, burned into my consciousness. Fantasies of survival remain as some of my clearest memories of early childhood, resurfacing in strange and unexpected ways.

EVENTUALLY, MY MOM learned to see my fevers coming. She knew how to read me, better than anyone else. She could see it in my eyes, feel it in her bones, and when I told her about my visions—those images of death and destruction—she held me and told me everything would be OK, that I was safe and nothing was going to happen. I believed her—even if it was a promise girded by faith rather than reason.

Mom was the only one who'd hang out with me when I got up early in the mornings, wakened from sweaty, troubled sleep. Often it was just the two of us in those quietly magical morning hours when the day was full of possibility and dreams. My time with her was quiet, careful, and peaceful. Never lonely. Even if we felt like the only people alive on the planet.

If she had gone off to work or out jogging, I'd grab my blanket and make my way back down to the basement. Every Saturday morning in the early '80s I turned on the old wood-cabinet Zenith and waited for the *Super Friends* television show. It came on at seven. At 6:30 was Orion Samuelson's *U.S. Farm Report*. Samuelson was a nice man who wore glasses and overalls and talked about rainfall, harvests, grain prices, and something called "pig futures."

Kansas City, 40 miles to the east, just past a small swath of farm country, was listed as a high-probability target for nuclear attack. Lawrence too. Part of this was because of the Titan missile sites near Wichita and the string of Minuteman silos just across the border, near Sedalia, Missouri. Part of it was because we were the so-called breadbasket of America, and the theory was that the Soviets would try to cripple our grain and food production by wiping out the crops and the railroads that hauled the grain and cows and pigs. Of course there's also Fort Riley, near Junction City, home of the U.S. Army's famed First Infantry Division, "the Big Red One," and a vast web of natural gas pipelines spreading across the state.

But most disturbing of all to me was the Wolf Creek nuclear power plant in New Strawn, Kansas, just seventy-five miles away from my family's house. I knew this. I didn't know then that if I had visited the plant with my parents, I might have been able to step inside the Dwight D. Eisenhower Learning Center and, with an advance appointment, participated in a nuclear power plant control room simulator. I could have pretended to contain a partial core meltdown and then perhaps stroll along the paved trails in the Wolf Creek Environmental Education Area.

THE TRUTH WAS that I needed the *Super Friends* as a kid. They kept me company those early Saturday mornings. They truly were my friends. But it was more than that. Thanks to the anxieties of the '70s and the subsequent Reagan administration, I was convinced that it was merely a matter of time before we all died a horrible, hairless death, and evil bald-headed men like Lex Luthor, with other assorted super-villains and freaks like Solomon Grundy, would rule the world.

I was afraid of the future, more comfortable with the fantastical, and there was even something very soothing about Orion Samuelson's *U.S. Farm Report* as a prelude to the real show, a homey, simple sort of feeling. There was a glow of anticipation surrounding the *U.S. Farm Report*, a hum of suspense in the haystacks-and-fake-barn set. There were true drama and tension in the teleprompted narration, the sleepy singsong voice of the host. I could barely wait, but I had to. Sit and wait. Sit and wait. Because soon, Lex Luthor, Bizarro Superman, Solomon Grundy, and the Legion of Doom would rise from the swamp—moss hanging from the eye sockets of their skull-shaped lair—and I would settle into an epic battle of good versus evil, where only mutant powers keep the world dancing along the thin line between normalcy and chaos.

The Three Mile China Island Syndrome 4.

THE BLOCKBUSTER 1979 movie *The China Syndrome*, starring Jane Fonda, Jack Lemmon, and a young, bearded Michael Douglas, tells the dramatic story of a near meltdown at a nuclear power plant and the subsequent conspiracy to cover up the accident.

It was released twelve days before March 28, when the Three Mile Island nuclear facility in Dauphin County, Pennsylvania, experienced a partial core meltdown of a pressurized water reactor, releasing into the atmosphere, among other things, thirteen million curies of what are called radioactive noble gases—colorless, odorless gases that quickly fill up empty spaces.

This synchronicity between fiction and reality was not an unusual coincidence. This was the sort of boundary-blurring experience that defined my childhood. The film even contained an eerie reference to the destruction of an area "the size of Pennsylvania."

Not only was the movie credited for contributing to much of the public panic surrounding the Three Mile Island accident, but it was also cited in several press conferences afterward when reporters and others had trouble understanding both the mechanics and magnitude of the potential disaster. That is, the movie—a dramatic fiction—became a reference text for objectively explaining the truth of the danger faced by millions of Americans.

I was six years old when *The China Syndrome* debuted in theaters, just nearing the end of my first year in grade school. I know that much. But for some odd reason much of the following year is absent from my memory, as if it had been wiped away, erased from my slate. While certain ages are defined by bright clear pictures and sharp memories, I can't even be sure of the name of my second-grade teacher. Was it Mrs. Harris? Did she have gray hair? Was she kind or harsh? I can't say.

This year of my life is mostly a fuzzy area between ages six and eight—though I also know that it was the first year of my life in which my fever hallucinations subsided and eventually faded away completely. I'd had my tonsils removed in first grade, and it was as if the doctors removed my sight too. I no longer saw visions of the apocalypse like I used to, but I was still afraid.

I recall my parents discussing Three Mile Island, but the event seemed very far away, both physically and emotionally, and I suppose it wasn't much of a real threat to Kansas—noble gases or not. I do, however, remember my dad talking a lot about the Wolf Creek nuclear power plant, about how it was safe and secure and different from Three Mile Island. He was fond of touting the clean and efficient nature of nuclear power. I learned about fission and fusion from Dad. Facts. Information. Statistics. That's how he tried to explain some of these things to me, how he tried to make me understand the mechanics and threat of nuclear power plants. But it did little to assuage my fears.

Siren Song

GROWING UP IN Kansas is to grow up with the threat and promise of devastation—if not by nuclear warheads or a reactor meltdown, then at the very least by a catastrophic tornado.

I've seen more tornadoes on television than I have in person—most of them recently on those storm-chaser TV shows. The only twister that hit Lawrence when I was a kid touched down in 1980, on the south side of town, damaging a few homes, ripping up a Kmart, and, of course, leveling a mobile-home park—places Dad always referred to as "tornado bait."

Some of my fear of tornadoes was tempered by my father's love of storms. Like most native Kansans, when the sky turned a soupy green and the clouds began to roil and tumble across the sky, tendrils reaching down, we didn't cower in a basement or a cellar. More often than not we'd stand out in the yard and stare up at the show. It wasn't uncommon to look up and down the street and see your neighbors in the same state of wonder and trepidation—all of us gawking at the spectacle.

I WAS NINE years old when the tornado hit Lawrence. We lived in a big house on a golf course, nothing like a mobile home, and most days I felt relatively safe there.

That didn't last long. After a valiant but ultimately doomed effort by his company to build solar-powered homes, my father's construction business collapsed into bankruptcy and the housing market bottomed out. In many ways, it felt like the end of our world—a sudden and precipitous fall from grace. I felt unmoored, adrift, and constantly in danger of capsizing.

We first moved from our large home, which my father had designed, to a tiny duplex, then to a battered house two blocks away from the elementary school that my younger brother, Matt, and I attended. It wasn't easy on the family, but we tried to make it work, tried to move forward. You could tell the whole thing had strained already tense threads between my parents.

We spent the summer remodeling the house—patching holes, painting, refinishing and replacing things, doing what we could to adapt. Dad got a new job selling stocks. Mom kept working at the church. Instead of boarding a bus every day, Matt and I walked through the water tower park and down the street to the school. We were too close for comfort. We could almost hear the shrill noise of children in the morning, the anguished creaking of bus brakes, or a teacher's whistle calling us inside.

Any of these sounds would have been better than some alternatives.

The school district held tornado drills once a month, it seemed. They began with a frightful cacophony. The big yellow siren mounted to the pole on the playground cranked up with a gut-shaking anguished howl, *wooooOOOOO,* causing bowels to quiver and knees to shake. The alarms inside the school made a loud guttural, bleating sound that rattled in my rib cage.

These sirens were the same sirens that would go off in case of an actual nuclear attack, and I could hear them from my basement bedroom where I hid out, read books about dogs and the Hardy Boys, and pretended that everything was OK with my family.

When the horns sounded at school, Mrs. Frakes would clap her hands together and announce, "Tornado drill, kids. Line up." We stood single-file against the wall. Then we had to march out of the room single-file and line up in the hallway.

Outside, the yellow siren rotated around the pole, howling, the noise coming at us in waves, *woooOOOOooo, wooooOOOOoooo.* We walked slowly out into the hall, following Mrs. Frakes, and lined up against the brick wall. Mr. Armstrong, the principal, strolled the hallways bellowing, "Heads between your knees! Heads between your knees!"

Mr. Armstrong had a square head and tinted square glasses with wire frames. His hair was a boxy helmet of brown. He wore brown suits and Hush Puppies. He looked like a toy man, a principal action figure. As he strutted up and down the hall, we assumed the position. I crammed my head between my knees, the rough denim of my Toughskins rubbing against my ears. I stared at my shoes, picking at bits of mud on the soles. I squeezed my knees against my ears. We had been taught that an incoming tornado sounds eerily like a freight train, and the noise was already unbelievably loud.

My father tells stories about the drills they ran through in school during the '50s—the same position, the same cacophony—but with a different threat, the threat of atomic bombs. He knows now how foolish it was to think that tucking your head between your knees would save you from the A-bomb, but back then their danger drills were infused with a dose of hope we didn't have growing up in the '80s. He actually believed they might survive. They all did.

Thirty years after Dad had sat like this in his elementary school in Greensburg, Kansas, there I was in Lawrence with my head between my knees, eyes on the floor, my senses muddled up—assuming the same position—surrounded by a sea of wailing and bleating sirens and the chattering murmur of children's voices. I tried to listen for that low, chugging rumble of a freight train, that white-noise roar of the storm.

At times I thought the tornado noise would be a welcome relief. I imagined the silence that would wash over the school if a real tornado were bearing down on us, and how that rumble and roar would slowly overwhelm all the other noise. Everyone would fall silent as the roof of Hillcrest School was peeled off and tossed into the air like a playing card, the black funnel twisting above, sucking children into its vortex, sucking the janitor and her dust mop up, Mr. Armstrong too, and all the other bullshit in the world. I was the only kid with my head up, the only one watching it all, the only witness as the school, the walls around us, began to disintegrate and the bricks flew like bullets, grass blades embedded in trees, and then a voice came at me, piercing the fog of my imagination.

"Church!" Mr. Armstrong bellowed. "Head between your knees!"

What's the point? I wanted to say. I lowered my head again, stared at my shoes, and closed my eyes. Waiting. *Foolish humans,* I thought. *We'll all be dead if a tornado hits the school. Don't you know that? You might as well enjoy it. Besides, if the twister doesn't get us, the bombs will. None of this makes a bit of difference.*

I was a big kid, fat-kneed and somber. I'd begun to grow, to take on the weight of the world. I hated Mr. Armstrong for not understanding how the apocalypse comes back, or how this life can grate on a family, or how the constant threat and promise of devastation can wear down even the most muscled hearts.

Cornflake Fallout

IN THE SUMMER of 1982, after years of tension, the apocalypse resurfaced for me. In those waning months before my sixth-grade year, the TV movie *The Day After* began filming in Lawrence, and I, for one, was convinced the world had truly tilted toward its rapid and inevitable demise.

Produced by ABC Motion Pictures and directed by Nicholas Meyer, of *Star Trek: The Wrath of Khan* fame, the movie made my hometown a star. The production crew and actors simulated the days after a nuclear attack on Middle America, leaving rubble and a fair amount of angst in their wake. They actually purchased the remains of a recently demolished apartment building in Topeka and trucked the bricks, pipes, drywall, and other rubble in, spreading it out on the streets of Lawrence for some scenes.

The movie was regularly promoted as something called "faction," a mix of fact and fiction; it somehow managed to take on the aura of truth and was often called a "realistic portrayal" of life in the days after the apocalypse.

This was problematic for so many reasons.

The filming was covered extensively in our local newspaper, *The Lawrence Journal-World*, in which there were regular interviews with people who had surrendered their homes or barns or businesses to the filmmakers. One family, the Wulfkuhles, let the ABC special-effects crew blow their barn to smithereens in exchange for a brand-new barn—never mind the odd visual logic of a barn exploding from the inside out when the story is that it has been leveled by waves of nuclear energy unleashed by a direct hit on Kansas City.

The interviews with older Lawrence citizens in both *The Journal-World* and national magazines like *Newsweek* and *Time* were often characterized by a pervasive sense of confusion over all the fuss—which of course only reinforced the producer's belief about the honest simplicity of Lawrence folk. Much of this was because, as extras and bit players in the movie, we only had a vague outline of the story. We knew that a lot of people were upset about the movie, but we couldn't have guessed the firestorm of publicity and attention it would generate one year later when it aired.

The film portrays a nuclear attack with direct hits on Kansas City and surrounding targets depicted in '80s-era special-effects extremity—missiles erupting from the prairie and giant mushroom clouds blooming in the blue sky.

Still today—though more rarely now—I will have someone remember my hometown as "that place that got nuked," when in fact Lawrence wasn't nuked at all. Lawrence served as a place of refuge in the film because it had the only hospital around. It was the place to which everyone was fleeing. It's often mistaken for the prime target. I blame this confusion partly on the fictional legacy of Kansas. To most people, it's a place that *should* get nuked—not because it's done anything wrong, but because in most of the national imagination Kansas is an abstraction, a symbol of nostalgic innocence, the kind of landscape where the end means something more.

Aside from what it said to us and about us as a town, the film also spoke to an entire generation of kids. It's a movie that most people of a certain age remember quite vividly—even if they have trouble conjuring up specific scenes from the film, even if the truth of it was a bit elusive, or even if their only memory is of not being allowed to watch it. *The Day After* is a movie with the subjective permanence of psychic injury—like the time you realized your parents were fallible or that the world was a dangerous place—and it occupies the strange place in American culture of a bad movie that is also a very important movie, or the kind of art that is deceptively, almost insidiously, significant.

ONE DAY DURING that summer—an unusually wet and rainy summer—I stood just down the street from the Big Brick Church, camped out on a familiar street corner with my parents and my brother, Matt. We waited. We fidgeted. We'd come to watch them film a scene, but we could barely imagine what was coming.

I felt as crispy and fragile as a paper house, thin-skinned and electrified. I was terrified of nuclear war. I knew I would bear witness to the carnage, watch the destruction unfold around us, stare and point. Hungry and impatient. Waiting for the show like everyone else. It was seductive. There's no point denying that. We were in the movies.

I'd heard stories of the producers paying people $75 to shave their heads into patchy approximations of radiation sickness and imagined myself lining up to take part. I'd heard about casting calls for extras and whispers about a local girl, Ellen Anthony, who had landed a role in the film. I'd heard strange tales of the crews purchasing piles of rubble from a demolished apartment building and spreading it over streets, treating it like treasured props.

On this particular day, the sign for our local downtown lingerie store, Undercover, had been repainted, altered, blurred for some reason—the pink storefront stained with dark smudges of soot. The picture windows were shattered into sharp teeth, bricks scattered across the sidewalk amid scraps of lumber, and several junked cars sprayed with clouds of black paint were parked out front. The store's mannequins had been stripped of their panties and bras, toppled, scattered, and posed in compromising positions. Normally lush trees out in front had been prematurely denuded of leaves, limbs hanging broken, trunks splintered, heartwood exposed.

A crowd had gathered, other families hooked arm in arm, slack-jawed and gawking. Photographers from the local paper snapped their shutters. We all wanted action and excitement. We wanted the Hollywood magic, the voyeuristic thrill of being "behind the scenes." Nearby, two industrial-sized yellow fans bolted to a flatbed tractor-trailer cranked to life. They hummed and whirred, blowing thick clouds of white flaky fallout into the air. The director, Nicholas Meyer, barked "ACTION," and the cameras began to roll. I watched it all from a safe distance. The white bits drifted down around us, clattering to the concrete like helicopter seeds in spring.

Dad picked up a piece of fallout matter and turned it over in his hand.

"What is it?" I asked, gazing up at him.

"Looks like cornflakes," he said, snapping the flake between his thumb and forefinger, "painted white."

Dad grinned at this thought, marveling at the make-believe.

"What a waste of cereal," Mom said. She was right.

The cameras rolled on, the scene slowed and burned into my brain, lingering there now for over twenty-five years. Jason Robards stumbled past the carnage—cornflakes fluttering around us all in a breakfast-cereal simulation of nuclear fallout.

Manageable Destruction

I ASKED MY MOM recently if she remembered why the filmmakers had chosen Lawrence for *The Day After*.

She said, "I think it had to do with the *manageable* size of the downtown street, and that this was to be an experience in small-town America."

Apparently it had nothing to do with me.

Lawrence did look like a movie set and is still, in many ways, identified with that mythic idea of a place untouched by influences from the outside, untarnished by the sins of cities and the excesses of pop culture—a kind of utopian vision. We were supposed to be so innocent, so clueless to the implications of what was happening, and so romanced by the appeal of Hollywood that we would be *manageable*. We were also supposed to be representative of a small town in the Midwest, a place with simple lives, simple values, and simple responses to the film.

Many people were, of course, openly opposed to the movie—or opposed to the nuclear-arms race. At least one outspoken protest group formed, calling itself "Let Lawrence Live," and its leader was a man who would later teach one of my anthropology courses. Seizing upon publicity from the movie, the group spoke out against nuclear proliferation and against the movie (sort of).

Their protest of the movie seems a bit misplaced to me, since by most accounts the movie was, if anything, a statement *against* nuclear proliferation. It takes some work to see any anti-communist, pro-nuke agenda in Meyer's movie, but I suppose it could be done.

When *The Day After* was filmed, Lawrence had a population of at least 50,000 citizens, a state university with an enrollment exceeding 20,000, and a world-renowned underground punk rock scene (centered primarily on a bar in the midst of a cornfield called the Outhouse and, to a lesser extent, places like the Bottleneck). It was also home to William S. Burroughs, the counterculture superhero. Burroughs lived on a ranch on the outskirts of town, where he took methadone and made art and then blasted it with a shotgun at his infamous parties.

LAWRENCE LIKED TO imagine itself as a fuzzy-soft small town, liked to sell itself that way from time to time, but we had our underbelly too. We weren't the rubes we appeared to be. But you can't sell this stuff to Hollywood unless maybe they're making a David Lynch film—which, of course, would probably have been more appropriate and much closer to my own Kansas movie. The winged monkeys of Oz would all land starring roles. They would speak in tongues and hang from the trees by their prehensile tails. They would be there with me in high school a few years later when I stood in the Burger King parking lot after playing a varsity basketball game and watched a mini-riot between twenty or more black athletes and white "hicks."

The monkeys would snicker over my shoulder as I innocently stuffed a Whopper into my mouth and witnessed seven black guys, some of them my teammates, in a circle kicking the living shit out of a kid from my drafting class. He would show up at school on Monday with his jaw wired shut and discover that it's even harder to use the n-word when you have to eat through a straw, and the monkeys would flap and hover over all of us, reminding us how hard it is to leave the past behind.

SOMETHING ELSE STRIKES me about Mom's memory of the filming. She doesn't seem to have any strong connection to the very real threat of nuclear war, the buildup of weapons in both the U.S. and the U.S.S.R.

She said, "I also couldn't quite connect with *why now*. Yes, the Cold War was still in our lives, but it really seemed so secondary to what I had experienced in the '50s, and the repercussions of Vietnam and the race riots were so much more in my mind."

This was true, of course. Mom had lived under the nuclear threat for most of her life. Like Dad, she'd seen the movies at school, drilled in the classroom for a possible atomic strike. She'd grown up in the shadow of Hiroshima and Nagasaki, gone to college during Vietnam. She'd lived through the assassinations of both Kennedys and Martin

Luther King Jr. and can pinpoint the places she was when she learned of their deaths. I can't really begrudge her for not internalizing the nuclear fear I felt in the '80s. It was more abstract, more existential and universal—less real in many ways.

Maybe it was too painful to think of her sons' futures that way. No parent wants to believe that her children will be dead before they grow up. Mom was busy raising two boys, working at the Big Brick Church, trying to survive in the world of our family, *and* expected to be fully in tune with the nuclear arms race.

Maybe I'm demanding too much when I think that she and Dad should be able to recall the angst of my generation. Or maybe that's exactly what it means to be members of different generations—you have radically different perceptions of the same reality.

Mom was just trying to make sense of a crazy world where she had to teach her children to live and prosper, a world where she was struggling to find her place too. Perhaps her memory has selected out some of this, filtered away the context a little bit—and I don't blame her for this. This is what we do. The stories we tell of our pasts are never objective, never mere recitations of fact. There's always a bit of fantasy.

I BELIEVE THAT the screenwriter, Edward Hume, probably chose Lawrence for the setting of *The Day After* partly because of the state of our state in the public consciousness, a landscape always associated with that gingham-clothed girl, Dorothy, her little dog too, and supernatural tornadoes—but a place also associated with tales of violent apocalypse.

Kansas is a symbol, a representation, a metaphor, and Lawrence seemed like the perfect new distillation of that. It was no longer the black-and-white world of *The Wizard of Oz*, but something more complicated. Besides that, Lawrence was willing to bend over backward to accommodate the production crews. We had a hospital, campus buildings, and schools that we were ready to open up for their use.

It makes a kind of easy narrative sense that Kansas would be subjected to a nuclear war, hopelessly scalded by an atomic blast, and reduced to a lawless wasteland.

How many times have you heard an action movie star say the words "We're not in Kansas anymore," or some version of this line from *The Wizard of Oz*?

Typically, this is said during a particularly sticky situation where it seems likely that the actor will die or be maimed severely, and it always refers to the extremity or absurdity of the situation. That is, Kansas is always presented as the opposite of anything extreme, absurd, dramatic, or remotely interesting. It's become a standard narrative flourish for screenwriters and advertising copywriters; it is regularly used in action flicks or science fiction movies.

THE ORIGINAL LINE is uttered by Dorothy as she steps out of the uprooted farmhouse into the vibrant, magical Technicolor land of the Munchkins, and it expresses her wonder and amazement at this new world. The sentiment of the original line is mostly positive. It reveals Dorothy's perception, however flawed, of this new world, and it still reinforces that idea of Kansas as a land of simple, stark contrast. Somehow Oz is more real, or at least more *alive*, than Kansas.

There was talk at the time of Lawrence becoming something of a small-town Midwestern Hollywood, a made-to-order set of wholesome-looking neighborhoods filled with ruby-cheeked youths and jolly round women wearing aprons, bearded men in flannel shirts and hordes of people willing to shave their heads for money or surrender their houses to production crews. Lawrence certainly appears innocent enough with its quaint tree-lined downtown and old Victorian homes, but it was at its core the kind of place willing to trade this image for others of nuclear devastation.

In the following years, two other movies were filmed in Lawrence: *Earth Girls Are Easy*, a bubblegum farce staring the eternally obnoxious Julie Brown; and *Kansas*, a film about young, handsome criminals on the lam that was shot, in part, in the old Eldridge Hotel, formerly the Free State Hotel and a building targeted in both the Sacking of Lawrence and Quantrill's raid. *Kansas* starred Matt Dillon, our "Dallas" from *The Outsiders*, a near cult hero to many teens for his role in a movie about small-town class conflict, violence, and misunderstood youth. Unfortunately, the movie *Kansas* was about as exciting as the title, and it did little to help the cause of promoting Lawrence.

There were no epic sagas. No gripping crime thrillers. No action flicks. No romantic comedies. No Oscar-winning actors. Just unsubstantiated rumors of Dillon trashing hotel rooms and screwing teenagers. Soon Hollywood realized that they could just make a fake

Lawrence in a warehouse or a back lot, and the production crews stopped coming—at least until recently.

The short-lived CBS TV series *Jericho* debuted in 2007 and again told the story of a small Kansas town trying to survive after an apparent nuclear attack on America. The show's production crews spent about a weekend in town, using some homes and businesses in North Lawrence as exterior shots for the show, gathering bits of texture to add to the authenticity of the vision. Starring Johnny Depp look-alike Skeet Ulrich, the show was canceled after one season. It did, however, develop a cult following that, with a kind of grassroots uprising, returned it on air for another season before the network finally killed it.

As usual, Lawrence was happy to accommodate the producers. If anything, our history reveals our sympathy for such stories, and they actually "renamed" North Lawrence "Jericho" for a day. It wasn't the public spectacle that *The Day After* was for us—perhaps because such nuclear threats now seem like ancient history, the antiquated peril of a Cold War few people even remember, or perhaps because we'd learned something from our experience with *The Day After* about the power of the imagination to reshape landscape and change the meaning of our home.

Preface to *Dahlberg Variations*

WHEN I WATCH *The Day After* now, I want to revise it. I want to make changes, updates, and additions: The boy, Danny Dahlberg, would make a superb voice-over narrator for the story. He's under-utilized as a character. The innocent farm boy, lost in the shadows of his gregarious older sisters; the boy who loves his father and his dog; the boy blinded by the blast, who spends most of the movie wearing a gauzy eye bandage. Danny is full of potential. He is our Tiresias, our blind oracle in the cave imparting riddles, half-truths, and murky lessons to wandering protagonists.

With some revision, some editing, the voice-over adult Danny could sound much like Daniel Stern on *The Wonder Years* or maybe Richard Dreyfuss from *Stand by Me*—with that nostalgia-laden tone of reflection and good humor, but tinged with a twenty-first-century dose of irony and cynicism. Later, he becomes an extreme version, a persona, a disembodied voice lingering in the margins of childhood, giving some humorous distance from the gravity of the events.

Adult Danny says things like, "On the day the world ended, I got a huge pimple," as we see him as a boy on-screen squeezing a zit into a mirror just as the ignition keys for the first warheads are inserted into a mysterious electronic panel.

He might say, "Here I am pumping water from the well, filling up jugs for one of Dad's crazy ideas," while on-screen the boy Danny pumps a red handle, methodically yanking it up and down, pouring water into a jug as the narrator continues, "I didn't understand why I had to fill every vessel in the house with water, but I knew it was important. I knew it mattered to my father."

He becomes the kind of guiding, patient voice we need, the character we most identify with, the one with whom we feel some kinship and bond—the silent boy in the corner of the cellar, his eyes swaddled in gauzy white cotton, ears listening to everything, understanding only fractions of the story behind the war; the boy who, if he could, might speak in grim tones about tensions between his parents, slight rifts in the bonds of their family, frustration at being ignored and underestimated by his siblings or a general inability to connect the dots, angst over his inability to see the relation between the narrative lines crisscrossing his life.

Like most of us, Danny doesn't understand war. He can't quite comprehend why we need to have nuclear weapons. He would be, in my revision, the sympathetic antiwar persona of the Midwest—just a boy growing up in a world that seems doomed, living in a place that feels like a rudely fabricated stage.

Danny is the kind of boy who talks obsessively about certain subjects, especially when he's nervous, and in the oppressive stink and silence of the storm cellar he mumbles about superheroes, reciting story lines from his favorite comic books or rambling on about recent episodes of *Super Friends*. We hear this on-screen—or, rather, we overhear it, just under the narrator's patient delivery of the day-to-day minutiae of his family.

The voice-over sounds good, strong, emotive, and patient, even corny sometimes. Danny says things like, "Dad and I had packed the cellar with canned food, much of it beans: green, pinto, lima, wax, black, red, and kidney. We didn't think about how that would change the atmosphere in the cellar."

The next shot shows the family sitting around the cellar with clothespins on their noses and a laugh track cues up, allowing us to guffaw along with the fake studio audience as the family farts uncontrollably.

In the worst of times, Danny's words rise over the chaos like a soft blanket. Perhaps tinged with an ironic, slightly sarcastic, and droll sense of humor, his narration shields us from the horror of the fallout and the piles of charred carcasses, allowing us—the audience—the soft luxury of psychic distance.

IN ONE IMAGINED scene, Danny sits in his pew in the decimated country church, and, as the preacher fades to background noise, he delivers a monologue of his own. Danny relieves us from the melodrama of the days after the bombs, perhaps even poking fun of the sentimental wailings of the man behind the podium, the man with his broken glasses. He says something like, "I never did like our preacher. He always went too far, never knew when to pull back and just be human. Even the green bean casserole at church functions was a 'gift from God,' a 'sacred offering,' or 'the body of Christ,' and he couldn't just appreciate french-fried onions for what they were—a topping to the slop."

Danny is a sympathetic narrator, a voice we can trust. He helps us connect the dots, and because his voice is the voice of an adult, we understand that he has survived, that he has lived to tell the story. He helps us remember that this is all artifice, fabrication, fiction, and not a documentary narrative of actual events. Perhaps, in my revision, he could invoke the infamous *War of the Worlds* broadcast, when Orson Welles was blamed for provoking mass pandemonium and suicides because he told a story that sounded too real, or perhaps Danny could pause amid the devastation to fill in the context, flesh out the history, and allow us to look away from the bright center into the penumbral regions of those days before the end.

Flea Market Memorials

JOHN BROWN HAD already swung from the gallows by the time the murderous Quantrill unleashed his own storm of violence on Lawrence, but I've always linked the two of them together in my mind, imagining them as opposing forces in an epic battle of good versus evil played out in my hometown.

Brown was one of the first Kansas heroes—or at least he was for me. The John Steuart Curry mural *Tragic Prelude*, originally painted in the Kansas State Capitol rotunda, always captivated me—and it still does. It's a terrifyingly beautiful image of the iconic man. It shows him as I want to imagine him.

Our elementary school took a field trip to Topeka every year, and, after we filed out of the yellow buses and made our way into the building, half-listening to the smiling capitol tour guide in the blue blazer, I'd stand agog before the image of Brown, absolutely mesmerized by his fury.

I'd always fixate on Brown's eyes, peeled wide and shocking white, his tiny hard pupils burning with insanity. His knee-length black jacket hangs down like a priest's cassock. Behind him a tornado spins on the horizon. Fires burn, smoke roiling over his shoulder. His hair stands up on end. His beard blows back as if some unseen force, some tide, is pushing against him. He appears larger than life, nearly twice as tall as the other men around him, and undeniably mythic. He looks like the sort of man capable of a massacre or a miracle. His anger was his power.

I liked to stand before the mural, my Marvel Comics lunch box clutched to my chest, and imagine living in the scene, a witness to the carnage, perhaps toting my own broadsword and unleashing some particularly gruesome vengeance on the illiterate slaveholding Missouri rubes.

I wanted to join Brown in the fight for freedom. I'd read all about the connections between events and people in Kansas history, the Civil War, Abraham Lincoln's presidency, and eventually even his assassination. I believed the story of Lawrence as the beating heart of Bleeding Kansas, a place of violent storms and refuge, a complicated and progressive place where the citizens kept their guns in a community armory, a place where the tensions beneath the Civil War played out early in particularly violent ways.

I also learned how in one skirmish south of Lawrence, near the Kansas–Missouri border, John Brown and a band of followers descended on a small community supposedly dominated by pro-slavery sympathizers. He and his men rode in on horseback, attacking the mostly defenseless farmers, hacking dozens of them to death with broadswords and machetes.

By most accounts, Brown was also a raving homicidal lunatic.

But he was *our* raving homicidal lunatic.

We loved him for the purity of his vision, for the intensity of his flame, and probably for seeing Kansas as the appropriate landscape for a religious war fought in the name of abolishing slavery. We loved him because he loved Kansas. We loved him for those historically "American" values of freedom and equality, with a dose of fundamentalism, that were used to justify every subsequent war.

Brown was an early extremist, a radical liberal before such categories existed, and he was also regularly described as a "guerrilla" fighter. Though he was hanged and buried by the time William Quantrill rode into Lawrence, we also loved John Brown because he seemed like the sort of protagonist we needed to fight an antagonist like Quantrill— the bogeyman of Lawrence history, the bad man who burned our town to the ground.

If only we could have resurrected the mythic Brown on that fateful day in 1863 and turned him into some kind of ten-foot-tall abolitionist zombie. Maybe the story of Lawrence would be one where John Brown and his army of anti-slavery undead feast on the brains of Quantrill's raiders . . . or maybe not.

Post-apocalyptic zombies might be going too far, but Kansas and Lawrence never really shrink from their violent past. It is simply reshaped, rewritten, archived, and drowned out with other stories. My other favorite memorial to John Brown can be enjoyed at the Free State Brewing Company in downtown Lawrence, where you can belly up to the bar and order a pint of John Brown Ale, and where you can also buy a T-shirt featuring an adaptation of Curry's *Tragic Prelude* mural, with Brown hoisting not a Bible, but an enormous mug of dark beer.

Despite his role as villain in the story of Lawrence, William Quantrill had his memorials too. One is the city seal itself, which features the smoldering ruins of Lawrence and a phoenix rising from the ashes. The other memorial is gone now, but it was a kind of sanctuary and sacred space for me and many boys like me.

It was called Quantrill's Flea Market, and the infamous criminal's likeness was painted on the limestone exterior, looming over the entrance. Centrally located in downtown Lawrence, Quantrill's Flea Market inhabited the basement of an old building that could have easily been torched by Quantrill himself during his homicidal rampage in 1863.

I spent a lot of time in Quantrill's quiet market space. I'd have my mom drop me off downtown on a Saturday or a Sunday after church, and I'd head straight for the dark basement, with its catacomb-like passages and its maze of knickknacks—shadowed and dank and full of meandering pathways. Part of my love for the place was the carnival atmosphere, the odd mishmash of antique toys, furniture, books, bikes, washtubs, clothes, and handicrafts. Part of it was the cheap soda and popcorn available at the flea market's snack bar.

My love was focused on the stall in a back corner where I used to paw through boxes and boxes of comic books, spending my meager allowance on copies of *Spider-Man*, *Daredevil*, and the occasional *Batman*. Mostly, though, it was *The X-Men*, my mutant heroes and their oracle-like teacher, Dr. Xavier, and *The Incredible Hulk*—both texts that featured complicated, angst-ridden, and afflicted heroes, mutants who were uniquely gifted for survival but who were also freaks and outcasts. It was then, when I was lost in these books, that I first began to imagine surviving the next decade.

I'd take my treasured comics home wrapped in plastic sleeves, clutching them tightly as I wandered past the antique furniture stalls—pausing perhaps to sit for a second on a chair from a matching living room set or to lie for a moment with my feet dangling off a double bed dressed in a lace spread.

I drifted through the model rooms, which were arranged as if people lived there in a strange sort of underground Victorian refugee camp—and part of me wanted nothing more than to stay there with them, sleeping in Quantrill's Flea Market, surrounded by history. I had my guidebook comics and my imagination, and this seemed like all I needed to survive.

The mural on the outside wall depicted William Quantrill almost like the sideshow entertainer Buffalo Bill Cody. He sported a handlebar mustache and a wide-brimmed yellow Stetson, a fringed jacket and crossed pistols—more campy cowboy than mass murderer, more friend than slaughterer of innocents, more character than creature. In the background of the picture . . . nothing much. Waving wheat. Bricks and paint. Crumbling mortar. In the foreground, the slowly fading image of evil.

The Mutants Shall Inherit

O NE INDISPUTABLE FACT about genetic mutation that I learned as a child was that it was often caused by exposure to nuclear waste or bomb blasts, and it spawned new heroes and new villains. The bomb destroys the human race, or the nuclear power plant nearby has a core meltdown, and it is a catastrophe; but it also ensures survival by creating new species—new and terrifying mutants and freaks who are uniquely suited to life in the new New World.

I first learned of wolf-ants from my cousin, Kathy, while we were still living in the big house on Alvamar Drive, right around the time that I was obsessively constructing models of survival. They lived in her imagination and, thanks to her stories, also in mine. She was older, wiser, and full of fantastical tales. But this one made a lot of sense to me.

Matt and I sat on the back porch swing, our legs dangling above the cement, and Kathy told us tales of the vicious, predatory creature that evolved, after the testing of an atomic bomb at a secret military base in the desert, into a mutant combination of fire ant and timber wolf. According to Kathy, the mutant wolf-ant had the furry body and muscled forelegs of a full-grown wolf—as well as canine speed, sight, and sense of smell—combined with the hard-shelled thorax and huge razor-sharp pincers of a giant mutant red ant.

They traveled in loose packs and dwelled in basements of suburban Kansas homes, building nests from blankets and pillows and the hides of family dogs. Wolf-ants were opportunistic hunters who ate nuts, berries, garbage, and cats, as well as their own young—not to mention slow-footed, sickly young boys. Kathy said, "A wolf-ant preys on the weak members of the pack."

The porch swing creaked.

Cicadas chattered in the grass.

Kathy kicked us higher and faster and Matt and I just held on tight.

I listened to my cousin, listened carefully to her stories of mutant beasts, and I *knew* they were all true. With my history of childhood illness and clumsy genes, I quickly realized that I was the perfect prey for wolf-ants. I began to see them in my dreams. They lurked in our basement and I heard their pincers snapping in the dark, *snip, snip, chicka, chicka, snip, snip,* combined with the eerie guttural howl of a wolf lungs, *howooooooo, woo, woooooo.*

I was terrified of wolf-ants.

But they made sense to me. I understood and respected them. I'd been nurtured on stories of abominations of nature. We all knew we were going to die horribly. It was just a matter of time. So of course much of our fantasy fiction and cartoons were about how we'd survive the apocalypse. And the key word here was "fantasy," because surviving it wasn't a reality—at least not surviving it in a form or identity that resembled the one we'd come to know. We understood intuitively that adaptation was the key to survival.

It's mutants who would inherit the earth.

As a nation, as a family, we were just beginning to recognize the legacy of pollution and toxic waste, just beginning to see that, while the human race as we know it might be wiped out, *life* would resurface, *life* would adapt and change. Mutation made sense. Mutation was normal.

I imagined myself surviving not by developing a hard carapace and pincers, not by mutating into some half-beast, but by adapting in more subtle ways, much like another one of my Saturday-morning cartoon heroes, Thundarr the Barbarian.

Of course, Thundarr was a Conan the Barbarian rip-off. He even looked like Conan and possessed the same Hulk-like eloquence with the English language. (This seems to be what largely defines a *hulk* or a *barbarian*—the inability to form complete sentences and the tendency to speak in dramatic generalizations. "Thundarr mad. Thundarr smash.") Still, I liked him. Thundarr carried himself with simple dignity. He not only survived, he thrived. Sure he was a "barbarian"— but he was perfectly adapted to his strange environment. He made friends and traveled extensively. He slept under the stars most nights and killed many bad mutants. He was both feared and respected by hordes of survivors. What more could you ask for?

I'm sure I wasn't the only boy who envisioned himself rising from the poisonous post-nuke atmosphere to ride a mutated horse-beast through a charred wasteland. (Was I?) I wasn't the only one who dreamed of wolf-ants and survival in a land where the Statue of Liberty had been toppled and half-buried in toxic sludge. (Was I?) This is why these cartoons were popular—because they spoke to a deep fear and a deep need in all of us, the need to mutate, adapt, and ultimately survive the apocalypse.

In my childhood imagination, survival was easy enough. After the bombs fell and the weak were vaporized, I figure I'd be just like Thundarr. I'd hook up with a super-hot sorceress princess and a fiercely loyal Chewbacca-like beast. We'd form a team of mutant heroes and travel the polluted planet fighting evil and the inevitable opportunistic profiteering mutants. We'd face half-men and half-animals, giant insects and carnivorous rats, and that two-faced mutant with his fancy helmet. We'd tangle with lizard people and massive meat-loving cockroaches.

It would be a hard life. But we'd persevere.

One day when the orange double sun of Earth scorched the planet and the soil cracked open, when a stiff breeze blew the hummingbird-sized flies off the horse-beasts, I'd meet my destiny—the legendary wolf-ant of the Plains.

Despite the ferocity of battle, we'd ultimately win the respect of the alpha wolf-ant, Raja, with our brazen displays of fearless aggression. Impressed with my leadership, my loincloth, my sword skills, and my obvious mercy for the injured wolf-ants, Raja would surrender his command and become my personal mutant wolf-ant steed. I'd affix a leather saddle to Raja's back and ride him into many righteous battles. We'd become legendary, my wolf-ant and I, and tales would spread of our great deeds, painted in grand strokes and vibrant colors on the copper cave walls of Lady Liberty's abandoned torso.

11

Extra Help

The Day After opens with a sweeping, panoramic shot of the Kansas countryside, the helicopter-mounted camera drifting over grain silos, red barns, ponds, and white country churches, and then the city of Lawrence itself, the University of Kansas campus with its signature red-tile roofs, Allen Fieldhouse and Memorial Stadium packed with fans for football. Then the film shows little snippets of life in Lawrence, snapshots of people going about their daily duties—innocent and simple people, the texture of life in the Midwest.

The producers of *The Day After* intentionally cast the movie with mostly local extras and actors to lend it a more realistic and authentic feeling, An opening shot of the film—what director Nicholas Meyer would describe to me later as a "fly on the wall" perspective—shows a teacher standing before a classroom full of children, many of them friends from school or church or sports leagues. Kids like me. Just like me.

It looks like they've filmed the scene in Pinckney Elementary, the old brick schoolhouse on 6th Street, but I can't be sure. I don't recognize the teacher, but the faces of the students press up against my consciousness. I know them but I don't. I see the outlines of familiarity—girls I might have dated once or dreamed of dating, boys I played Little League with or who were in my Boy Scout troop. But there is only one kid that I recognize right away.

I see Kendall Meade in the back, the skinny boy who would become my friend, my teammate in basketball, football, and track—the boy who would seem to defy gravity in the long jump and the 100-yard dash, when his legs moved cartoon-fast as he wheeled around the cinder-coated track.

Kendall would play running back to my tight end during our sophomore year of football, the year when all I had to do was get a shoulder into the defensive end to spring him on the outside. I'd hit my man, count to two, and look over my right shoulder to see Kendall racing down the sideline, disappearing behind a crowd of helmets. He was so fast he looked like he was flying. Kendall seemed almost superhuman to me at times—perhaps because I was a boy who always felt burdened by my body and the weight of fears.

When I found Kendall in the movie twenty-five years later, his image lit up on my computer screen, his slightly pixilated eyes peering out at me, I thought of the scar I'd seen on his chest one day as we dressed in the locker room after football practice—a long, puffy band of light-colored flesh that stretched the length of his sternum.

"How'd you get that?" I asked.

He looked down as if he didn't know what I was talking about and ran a finger down the length of it.

"Heart surgery," he said. "I was just a baby."

He was barely alive before they had to open up his chest and fix his heart. Kendall didn't remember them tinkering and didn't feel any different from anyone else, but he was always one of the kindest, most gentle, and happy people I ever knew, and I wondered if maybe when the doctors were in there they hadn't given Kendall something extra to help him survive.

NATHAN BERG MIGHT have been in that scene too, seated in that classroom. It's hard to discern faces sometimes. But he'd been an extra in the film and had several relatively extended scenes. Nathan had already done voice-over acting for the cartoon character Jeffy from an animated *Family Circus* TV special—a legend that was passed around elementary-school playgrounds long before I actually met him. Even as a kid, his reputation preceded him. He was, according to many people, a musical genius, a prodigy on the standup bass.

"You should see his hands move," they would say.

My first memory of hearing Nathan Berg play bass guitar was when he unleashed a particularly stunning solo on an acoustic upright bass during the West Junior High talent show in 1984, one year after *The Day After* aired. It was an experience that almost inspired me to cut off my finely cultivated mullet, discard my skin-tight parachute pants, and purchase some jazz albums.

I say "almost" because, unfortunately for Nathan, his solo was followed by another band performing a cover of Led Zeppelin's "Whole

Lotta Love" that featured a fat kid named Grims beating the crap out of a snare drum and knocking a cymbal stand over, while the lead singer did his best Glenn Danzig impersonation of Robert Plant. For a metal-head wannabe like me, Nathan's sublime bass stylings couldn't compete with this unfettered expression of pure adrenalin-fueled cock rock.

In high school, Nathan just disappeared. One day he was there. The next he had left to attend college early and study music on some kind of special scholarship. Eventually I would hear that Nathan, at the age of eighteen, was touring with Maynard Ferguson's jazz band and releasing his own solo album.

When I was eighteen, I still wore braces and was still trying to figure out who I was. Barely stumbling out of high school, I felt trapped by Lawrence. Until I found the world of ideas in college, I had a hard time picturing myself in any other place. I couldn't have imagined how I might look back on my hometown through the lens of this movie, or how the faces of Nathan and others would resurface again and again.

MEMORIES OF LIVING through *The Day After* are the kind that linger, rise, and imprint themselves permanently in my mind. When I tracked him down, Nathan recalled for me a scene at a casting call in Allen Fieldhouse, the famous basketball arena on campus where the film crew staged a large refugee camp scene featuring hordes of local extras who'd been paid to shave their heads into wispy approximations of hair and cover their faces with fake wounds. Nathan said that at the casting call, someone in the crowd asked about the rationale for choosing Lawrence as the setting for the movie.

A casting agent from the movie production solemnly explained that we were in the middle of the country and would be a likely target for high-radiation, high-dispersion atomic bombs that would contaminate agricultural products, poisoning the breadbasket of the nation and wiping out herds of cattle.

Nathan said, "The casting guy then asked all members of the press to identify themselves, and he said, 'I don't want any of that in print. Do you understand? None of it . . . ' He got kind of aggressive and took an intimidating tone toward the reporters.

"I thought about that in bed at night for weeks," Nathan continued.

What struck him was how deadly serious the guy was, as if this information was top secret and had to be kept on the hush-hush, or as if he'd made some PR faux pas and was worried he might ruin the shoot or spoil the simple innocence of Lawrence townsfolk. You had to wonder.

"Maybe he was just wrong and knew he couldn't back it up, or was worried what the investors would think . . . But his insistence to many in the room seemed like an L.A. oracle telling us Kansans about a big joke that was on us—*You're the target, man!!!*"

Nathan told me of another casting call for a scene filmed on the K-10 highway between Lawrence and Kansas City, where cars are disabled by the blast's electromagnetic pulse and refugees trudge along the side of the road. In the script, a soldier searching for his wife and child asks about his hometown of Sedalia, Missouri, and a voice from the crowd of refugees responds, "There ain't no Sedalia no more." That's the line. Just that one sentence. Everyone traipsed in front of the director and casting agents and repeated the line. But something wasn't right.

Nathan remembered, "The director didn't like how urbane and sophisticated all the Kansas actors sounded and encouraged them to ham it up and sound more like a good old boy. My mother and I joked about this for months and years afterward, doing our best Gomer voices. There was implicit pride that we were much cooler than these big-ego L.A. types gave us credit for."

Even the people most intimately involved with the filming understood that we were the subject of art and not actual participants in the art.

"Ham it up a bit, will you?" they said to our entire town.

This happens all the time in fiction. Characters are typecast, flat, and superficial. But the problem is that everyone involved in the picture—from Brandon Stoddard to Nicholas Meyer to Edward Hume to the chamber of commerce—all said that the reason the story was set and filmed in Lawrence was because of the authenticity of the people, because of the honest reality of our simple Midwestern lives.

IT'S FITTING PERHAPS that my very first memory of Nathan Berg is a memory also connected to his hands, those vessels of identity and control. It's a simple quiet sort of memory—the kind that seems to get forgotten in the nuclear wash of the '80s.

Nathan and I participated in tryouts for the competitive Little League Saints baseball team in Lawrence. We each failed to make the cut. Instead, we joined a city league and played on a team dubbed the "Radars."

Our uniform colors were purple and white, and we were a ragtag assortment of mediocre baseball players who played in the *other* lower "non-competitive" league. None of us really knew what the heck a "Radar" was, but I think it had something to do with the fact that one of the kid's dads was a radiologist and had sponsored the team.

The truth was that we probably looked like a whole team of Radar O'Reillys, and we couldn't have picked a better team name. I remember being a lot more excited about my uniform than I was about actually playing the games—which were mostly exercises in tedium combined with rare and fleeting flashes of excitement when one of the better boys actually hit the ball past the infield.

The coach put Nathan and me both in spots on the field where there weren't a lot of balls hit. I was at third base and stood out like a sore thumb. Most of the time, I just wanted to hide. The balls were hit mainly to the shortstop, the second baseman, the first baseman, the pitcher, and a few to the center fielder. And I was glad for this. I had no real desire to succeed in baseball. I wasn't the only kid like this on the team. There was a reason we were playing for the Radars. We stunk. Most of us could barely make contact with the ball and would have probably done better hitting it off of a fixed tee. Even our sporting equipment was half-assed, hand-me-down and second-rate.

I had a baseball glove made by the shoe company Pony and it said Pony in big white letters on a blue patch on the padded thumb. I got it at Gibson's discount center. It was garish and cheap. But nobody else had a Pony mitt and I convinced myself that this made me unique and cool.

Nathan Berg, however, had a baseball mitt that trumped all others in originality, one he claimed he had inherited from his father. It was red, white, and blue, each finger painted in alternating colors from Old Glory. I don't remember if it had stars painted on it too, but it was still spectacular.

Nathan got stuck out in right field, where he was all but guaranteed to spend most of the game standing by himself, far away from the crowd, the other players, the dirt infield, and sounds of the sparse fans. He paced and danced around out there in his saggy white pants, bright purple shirt, purple hat riding high on his head, and this glove, this gloriously odd and memorable mitt—a large patriotic leather glove in red, white, and blue, garish as a bomb-pop ice cream treat, lurid as a candy-coated confection.

Despite the fact that I teased him unmercifully about it, I was secretly quite jealous of his mitt and found it exotic, bizarre, and strange—sort of like jazz—but trimmed with the garish colors of America. Night after night, game after game, I stared in awe as Nathan stood out there in the misty blue-green grass and weeds, beneath the quivering lights, swatting at mosquitoes in the summer breeze, innocently waving the flag like a good citizen.

As I watched *The Day After* again from over two decades in the distance, I thought of Nathan and his hands, Kendall and his legs, his smile, and his bionic heart. I thought of them both when the bombs hit and vaporized the classroom full of children, reducing them to ash and rubble, and I wondered again how to survive such things.

12

Hulk Dreams

*T*he *Incredible Hulk, The Wizard of Oz, The Amityville Horror, The Day After, Nightmare on Elm Street,* and *Raiders of the Lost Ark* all make Joanne Cantor's list of the most psychologically disturbing movies and TV shows.

Cantor is a noted researcher and writer on the subject of media influence on children. In a piece titled "The Media and Children's Fear, Anxieties, and Perceptions of Danger," from the *Handbook of Children and the Media*, she talks about the potentially deleterious effects of TV violence, danger, or other graphic content on the emotional and mental well-being of children, both in the short and the long term.

Cantor's list of psychologically disturbing movies or television shows matches up pretty well with my greatest hits list of the '80s, and I wasn't surprised to see *The Day After* tagged with the others.

Raiders of the Lost Ark seemed an odd inclusion to me until Cantor mentioned the snake scene in the tomb, and I remembered how much that messed with my head and induced a visceral fear response to snakes that still remains in part today. My sister-in-law will cite a movie, *Slither*, as the single source of her overwhelming fear of snakes.

That scene in *Raiders*, combined with the skin-melting, apocalyptic wind-of-God scene at the end of the same movie, became my paradigm for scary movie scenes, everything else measured against it for years to come. When I imagined what a nuclear bomb would do to a human body, the pictures in my head looked a lot like the images of the melting Nazis when they open the Ark of the Covenant.

As troubling as it may sound, the Incredible Hulk was also a kind of role model for me. I collected the comic books as a boy and watched with much anticipation every week the network TV series based on his story, which aired weekly from 1978 until 1982—the year filming began on *The Day After*. David Banner, played admirably by Bill Bixby, was the quiet, unassuming scientist, the loner and drifter, a nice guy like me, a pushover even. Until you made him angry.

That was always a mistake. That's when the mutant took over and things got really messy.

The show, of course, ended each week with what I believe to be one of the most memorable and deeply sad final scenes of any television show ever produced—David Banner walking alone down a two-lane highway, faded denim jacket under one arm, duffel bag over his shoulder, his thumb in the air, and that melancholic piano music tinkling in the background.

It was awful.

I wanted to cry every single time I witnessed it.

As much as I loved *The Incredible Hulk*, the show also gave me horrific nightmares—the sweaty, violent kind that woke me up and kept me awake, afraid to drift back into that world. It was one of the first television shows that I deeply loved but that also seriously troubled me.

The Hulk himself was a near-constant presence in my dreams during those years, though not always malevolent toward me, and not in the way that my fever dreams felt. Sometimes I was just in the room when his temper exploded and he became the Hulk, and it was like sitting in closet and watching a grenade go off.

Sometimes I was David Banner, watching helplessly as my family died and I could do nothing to save them. Other times it felt like I was the Hulk, the angry one smashing furniture and trashing evil in the name of justice or vengeance or just existential angst.

I had trouble sleeping, but I was afraid to admit to my parents that the Hulk gave me nightmares. Sometimes I would stay up all night reading because I didn't want to sleep. I was nine years old, too old for that baby stuff, and I knew if I told them about the dreams they'd probably never let me watch the show again. So I kept watching week after week until the nights in which I didn't have nightmares got fewer and farther between. Eventually I couldn't take it any longer and confessed to my parents that the Hulk was tormenting me. We sort of decided together that maybe I should take a break from the show, just for a little while.

I skipped one episode and the nightmares stopped.

I was so pissed off. I wanted to watch *The Incredible Hulk*. I loved the show, but part of my psyche didn't agree. Part of my brain hated the Hulk. It was a subconscious, physiological fear response; it was nothing I could control, but something I had trouble accepting nonetheless.

I think the same is true for me and other movies, other images. I should just learn how to switch them off.

Turning off the TV is what Cantor would probably call a necessary "behavioral coping mechanism" when faced with potentially disturbing images. She says that in a few extreme examples, "acute and disabling anxiety states enduring several days to several weeks or more (some necessitating hospitalization) are said to have been precipitated by the viewing of horror movies such as *The Exorcist, Invasion of the Body Snatchers*, and *Ghostwatch*." I couldn't help but wonder if these acute and disabling states of anxiety could last for decades too. Something like that had come over me in the early '80s and never left.

Whether she's talking about *The Day After* or not, Cantor also mentions that in a 1981 survey, 40 percent of parents of preschoolers spontaneously mentioned *The Incredible Hulk* as a television show that significantly frightened their children.

I read this and—aside from worrying about parents who let their preschoolers watch *The Incredible Hulk*—wondered what it was that scared them so. Perhaps it was simply the power of the image—that big green angry hulk of a man. Maybe it was the bellowing, the violence, or the idea of metamorphosis. I wondered if it was the same thing that scared me—the realization that the Hulk was simply an extreme expression of an angry, chaotic core inside each of us.

13

Monkeys in the Trees

IN MY OZ, the winged monkeys hop and snicker and incessantly preen their greasy black wings. They've developed bad habits. They bow and dance when the Wicked Witch comes near, acting coy and obedient. But it is cold and dark in the margins of the castle, the anterooms where the witch makes them sleep, and when she leaves the room, they ape her movements with exaggerated gestures and a cacophony of barking. They piss in the corner and chuck feces at the door.

None of this surprises or impresses Dorothy. She thinks of herself as a friend of animals—but mostly of well-behaved animals. These monkeys are bad monkeys. Toto cowers and quivers in her lap, occasionally yipping if a monkey comes too close, but he knows his place. He is a good dog. The witch has assigned the monkeys to look after Dorothy, to make sure she doesn't escape. They are just doing their job, the witch's bidding.

One of the monkeys, an old one with tattered wings and large testicles that drag on the floor, appears drunk on fermented apples. He staggers over to Dorothy. Toto yips and growls, but, when the old monkey gets too close, Dorothy just takes off one of her ruby slippers and clubs him on the snout.

"Bad monkey!" she says, and the drunken monkey limps off to a corner, pawing at his nose.

"Hey, monkeys," Dorothy calls out. Rubbing her feet, she asks, "Can any of you speak sign language?" She repeats the question in ASL, a skill she learned from her mother, back home in Kansas.

One of the monkeys, a big one with a long gray beard and prodigious ears that they call Dr. Greybeard, signs back, "What do you want, human? The witch would turn us into toads for speaking with you."

"Oh good, a smart one," Dorothy signs. "You look like a leader."

Dr. Greybeard stiffens a bit, sits up a little more straight, looking proud.

In the silence of the castle, a bond is formed.

"I think we can get out of here," Dorothy signs, "all of us." She gestures at Toto and the room full of squatting monkeys, some of them smoking Pall Malls, most of them wearing dirty red vests and looking terribly depressed.

"Why would we leave?" Dr. Greybeard asks. "The witch feeds us loads of bananas, and she gave us these wings." He spreads his big greasy black wings and adjusts the tiny hat on his head. Dorothy can see where the chinstrap has rubbed his skin pink and raw.

She reaches out to him instinctively, brushing the worn flesh with the back of her hand. "Yes, but you're slaves. You're prisoners, mere workers for her bourgeois elitism. Don't you want self-rule? Don't you want democracy?"

The monkey turns away, curls inward for a moment, strokes his chin and scratches vigorously at his testicles. He tugs at his ears and shakes his head. He gazes around the room at his sad depleted band of chimps—many of them addicted to nicotine or sour apples, some having trouble adjusting to their wings and not sleeping well at all.

"What do you have in mind?" Dr. Greybeard signs.

Dorothy tells him of her plan to spirit them away from the witch's castle. She makes vague promises of a glorious life of bounty and excess in the tropical jungles of Kansas, a progressive, democratic land of individual freedom that has, since before the Civil War, been staunchly anti-slavery.

"Go on," he signs.

She paints a picture of farmland utopia, a metaphorical breadbasket. She tells him about the rivers and the trees down by the creek and truckloads of bananas. She tells him that walnuts grow on trees there. It all sounds good, but she's not convincing him. She can tell he wants something else, some other kind of sacrifice.

"What is it?" she asks, rubbing a hand into her eye and straightening her dress.

"The dog," Dr. Greybeard signs, pointing at Toto. "I've always wanted a pet."

Dorothy mulls over the situation. She strokes Toto's fur somewhat absentmindedly. Despite her gingham and innocent pigtails, she's always harbored resentment toward Toto for landing them here in the first place. If she's honest with herself, she can admit that. If she hadn't run after the damn dog, she might have made it into the shelter. She might never have landed in Oz. If he had been better behaved she'd still be home.

She wants to get back home. Kansas may be black and white and all bottled up, but she has a date with the captain of the football team. *You can see his collarbones, for god's sake, and all the tendons in his neck. His hands are the size of catcher's mitts—soft leather catcher's mitts.* She thinks how warm it must be in his arms. She thinks about her uncle, his broad shoulders and stoic chin, those damn overalls he's always wearing. She sees her aunt nervously wiping her hands on an apron Dorothy made in home-economics class.

She kisses Toto on the head, whispers "I'm sorry," and hands him over.

The little dog whimpers as Dr. Greybeard holds him up close to his chest, cooing and stroking his fur. The scene is so sweet and innocent—like something you'd see photographed in *National Geographic*—and it immediately convinces Dr. Greybeard to help Dorothy. He squawks and barks at his fellow winged monkeys and the message is spread to the masses with Dorothy's promises ballooning out, expanding into mythical tales of the Kansas jungles practically stinking of bananas and freedom.

Soon, after the Wicked Witch has fallen asleep for the night, the winged monkeys gather up Dorothy and Toto and carry them out of the castle in a mad flapping cacophony of wings. The witch, awakened from her sleep, her hair a wreck of tangles, rushes to a balcony and screams "Traitors!" as they flap through the greenish sky, lift up over the mountains, into the land of the East and the harmless little Munchkins.

Dorothy is delivered beyond them, back home to Kansas.

Later, when she has some trouble providing bananas, Dr. Greybeard eats Toto, and, fed up with Dorothy's empty promises, his band of evil minions disperses into the woods around Clinton Reservoir, just west of Lawrence. Decades of inbreeding and warring leave behind a tribe of feral winged monkeys that haunt the residents of Lawrence, taking up residence for much of the '80s in the rafters of City Hall and the upper reaches of church steeples. At night, they roost outside the windows of fearful young boys, and the silent movement of their hand-talking casts frantic shadow puppets on the walls inside. If they could whisper, they might've warned of coming storms.

The Day Before

14

O N M A Y 4, 2007, my obsession with the apocalypse, both real and imagined, began to crystallize into something like a purpose.

My wife was just a month or so pregnant with our daughter—that similar fluttering mass of cells—when I got a call from my dad.

"Have you seen the news?" Dad asked.

"No," I confessed. "Why?" I live in California now, and most days Kansas feels like another planet.

"It's Greensburg," he said. This was my father's hometown, the closest thing to an ancestral home we had.

"A tornado hit last night, and it's gone."

"What do you mean, gone?"

"I mean Greensburg is gone. Ninety-five percent of the structures were destroyed. Your Aunt Judy is OK. Her house is still standing. But your grandparents' old house is just completely gone. All the schools too. They're just rubble."

I paused to make sense of this, but I knew immediately that I would have to go home and see it for myself. I knew that I would have to try to somehow make sense of this legacy for me, my father, and perhaps my own children.

HERE IS WHAT I knew: Just after 9:00 p.m. (CST), a massive F5 tornado a mile and a half wide with wind speeds over 250 mph touched down south of Greensburg. Moving slowly, it plowed into the south side of town and churned through the heart of the community, destroying or severely damaging most structures, including the entire downtown business district, all three schools, and over 900 homes. Cars were tossed around like toys and mobile homes where blown to bits. All the schools and churches were destroyed. Most trees were completely stripped of limbs, leaves, and bark. Only a handful of houses on the eastern edge of town survived untouched. The tiny

airport—basically a cluster of Quonset huts and a strip of asphalt—
survived with minimal damage.

I CAME HOME six weeks after the storm and, before we went to see
Greensburg, Dad and I spent the day at a lake outside of Lawrence,
relaxing, enjoying the sun and the water, taking shelter in the shade of
the huge cottonwoods. It was hot already, starting to steam and bake.
The next morning we'd drive west, hoping to find something in the
post-tornado wake, hoping the weather reports weren't true and there
wasn't another F5 brewing on the High Plains.

Dad and I walked over to the swimming beach to float and wiggle
our toes in the mud. He waded into the deeper water and bobbed on
an inflatable tube. I joined him there and we talked about Greensburg,
especially the things he saw when he visited a couple of weeks earlier.

"They had this lot full of smashed-up cars," he said. "Each one of
them had a number spray-painted on the side. You know, like 2, 5, 6,
11, and so forth."

"Yeah?" I asked, paddling my feet in the water.

"Yeah," he said, "and you know what the numbers were for?"

"What?"

"The number of miles that car traveled in the tornado."

"Holy shit," I said.

"Yeah," he said. "That thing picked up cars and carried them for
miles."

"That's almost unbelievable."

"South of town, we saw where a mobile home had been picked up,
carried across the road, and dropped in the neighbor's front yard."

Dad had a lot of stories about Greensburg and the aftermath of the
storm, and we went through several of them—his tone a mixture of
awe and nostalgia—before he told me what was really on his mind. It
took a while, but we finally talked about his impending layoff from a
local excavation company.

"It stinks," he said. "But they didn't have a choice."

We floated in the water and talked about his job, where he spent his
days in a mobile trailer, running an asphalt plant, crapping in a portable toilet, hauling around rock and his 260-pound frame, a day-to-
day grind that he described to me as requiring "the top of my physical
abilities and the bottom of my mental abilities."

The truth is that he needed this job and this salary with an eleven-year-old son, my half-brother, still in elementary school, college looming on the horizon. But the job was yanked from beneath him by a man he considers a good friend, a man who really didn't have a choice. The once-booming new-housing market in Lawrence bottomed out, and, as Dad said, "If they aren't cutting streets, I don't have a job."

Dad blamed "no-growth" policies and developers who throw up acres of crappy apartments, sapping customers from suburban locales. But he knew it wasn't that simple. Nothing is simple, though sometimes it seems that the world works in strange repetitive patterns. When I was in elementary school, Dad had to recover once before when his business failed and we lost our house. Now he had to do it again.

He said, "I'm tired of starting over," and paddled his hands in the green water. "I'm too old for this."

He was right. Dad was old enough to retire, though retirement wasn't in his blood. He would probably go crazy if he wasn't working on something. Besides that, he had an adolescent son twenty-four years younger than me, another boy in the world, a brother I've barely known as such, and another mouth to feed, a mind to mold.

Dad probably wasn't obsessed with the idea of apocalypse, the end of one reality, the beginning of another. He was probably thinking about how he was going to pay tuition for my little brother at the private school in town.

Maybe because it was hard for me to think about my dad facing some of the same challenges I was facing, I couldn't stop thinking about the end of the world and what we might see the next day or two in Greensburg. I wondered if it would confirm my fears of youth, if it would bring back the terror and angst of the '80s and provide a kind of echo chamber—bouncing back the sounds and images of apocalypse that I had only imagined or barely remembered.

I couldn't stop dwelling on the mutant in each of us, that small part of my father that allows him to adapt, adjust, and change jobs, careers, and identities as much as anyone I know. My mother has this too, this tendency. Four different universities, experience in nearly every single aspect of student affairs. Three husbands now. Absentee parents. She and my father, each in his and her own way, have always adapted, changed, mutated in the face of challenges.

I must have known this for sure when my parents survived the death of my younger brother, Matt, in a car accident in 1992—each finding a way to live with that loss, to swallow it and grow a thick exoskeleton, a shell, a place to hide and recover. And I think I must have this ability too, some mutant tendency, a survival instinct I hope to pass on to my children. My wife, Rachel, has it too, maybe because she also lived through divorce and the crazy '80s and, more recently, the death of her aunt and her father to cancer.

We've lived in five houses and three states in my son's first six years of life. We've bounced around, searching for a home and job that fits, adapting to new environments—city, country, Colorado, Rhode Island, California. As a family, it seems like the only constants for us have been these tiny catastrophes and the presence of one another through it all. Some days I think we're postponing the inevitable return to Kansas, just circling around, waiting to land someplace like home. Other times I think home is gone, wiped away, eroded in the waves of history and distance that separate us.

BOOK 2 *THE END*

Downtown Lawrence, 1982

The most important movie we or anyone else ever made.

——Brandon Stoddard
President, ABC Motion Pictures, 1983
Referring to *The Day After*

DAHLBERG VARIATION

Danny wants to help his father prepare for the war. He sits on the porch of the farmhouse early in the morning, before anyone has risen for the day. Even his father still sleeps. Danny listens to the sparrows and chickadees crank up in the elms and watches the bats dart and dip, twirling their way back into the barn for the day. He sits there and wonders what the bomb will sound like when it does eventually come.

He thinks it must sound something like a tornado when the bombs hit, but he doesn't know for sure. They say a tornado sounds like a freight train, but Danny doesn't really know about that either. He can only imagine, and some days it seems like he's the only one who bothers to do so. Everyone else around seems so focused on superficial things. Wedding dresses. Diaphragms. Or whatever that thing is his older sister, Denise, keeps in her purse, that thing Joleen was telling him about earlier this morning, saying how she was going to steal it and hide it from Denise. He doesn't care about that stuff, doesn't really care much for Denise's fiancé, Bruce, either, or whether the two of them will ever have babies. He doesn't care if Bruce has "the most gorgeous blond curls" in the world, according to Joleen, or if he is a "dream" or any of that mushy stuff.

Danny wears his blond hair in a bowl cut and wishes he could just buzz it off like the other boys his age. His mother won't let him do it yet. "Your sister will be married tomorrow," she said at breakfast. "You don't want to look like a hoodlum, do you?"

Maybe he does want to look like a hoodlum. Maybe nobody will be getting married tomorrow.

His father, Jim, promises that someday he'll take Danny to the barbershop downtown, and they'll sit next to each other in the chairs and he'll let Rex give him a cool flattop, the kind Jim used to wear when he was a boy growing up in rural Kansas in the '50s and early '60s. He tells Danny about that time and about the round flat cans of butch wax he used to sculpt his flattop, and Danny thinks this sounds exactly like the sort of haircut he wants.

Danny knows now, though, that none of this may ever happen.

There may never be a barbershop.

Danny wants to tell Joleen and his mother that none of them may ever have hair again. He's heard the talk at school, the whispers about how radiation makes it all fall out, makes your teeth rot, your skin break out in festering sores. He wants to tell them that Bruce and his stupid motor-cycle won't mean shit after the bombs. But he doesn't. He just keeps his mouth shut like his dad taught him.

Later in the morning, Jim and Danny drive to town and it's just crazy with people everywhere, buying up all the food and supplies. They stop at the IGA and buy a whole flat of canned tomatoes and six big jars of peanut butter, taking the last ones from the shelf. The place is just mad with the crush of panicked people. He and Jim hustle out of there, take the food home and put it all down in the cellar, lining the shelves with nonperishables.

His father doesn't say much at all, doesn't offer platitudes or false hope; Danny appreciates this. Jim doesn't talk about hair or the wed-ding. He doesn't talk much at all. Danny understands the meaning in this silence, this lack of humor, the grim lines carved into Jim's face, and he realizes that this is no drill, no joke. His mother. His sisters. They just want to pretend it's not happening. But Danny knows—because he knows his father—that this is serious, that the end is here.

Danny is still working out in the yard, still trying to help, filling jugs with water from the pump when the first missiles rise from the horizon. He stops, stares, his mouth spread into a wide oval. Jim yells at him from the porch, "Get in here!", and Danny runs for the house. But the dog is loose in the yard and Danny goes back for her, running toward the blast. He loves that dog. He runs hard for her, trips and stumbles to the ground. Jim grabs him, screams at him, "Danny, cover your eyes!" But Danny can't stop from staring as the first warhead airbursts over Kansas City, a bright yellow blast and orange color spreading out to the edges of the horizon, pulsing and burning, a roiling black mushroom cloud rising up, billowing into the sky. The light fills his eyes and, for a second, feels warm and gentle like the sun in the afternoon warming his eyelids. But then it moves quickly beyond, pulsing and shooting hot stabs of pain until the picture begins to curl and fade and turn to black. Soon he sees nothing. Soon he will hear everything.

Danny Dahlberg had always possessed a terribly active imagination. He'd learned at an early age to find solace in his own mind, and he could spend hours, it seemed to his sisters, just playing alone in his room. Now, in the days after the bombs, he is forced to rely on four of his five senses. His eyes are gone, burned out by the light, but pictures keep rising up to the surface of his conscious mind as his hearing grows stronger and stronger. He still sees. But it is only of the past. All he knows of the new world is what he hears and feels.

Danny cannot see the cramped confines of the cellar where they have all taken refuge, though he knows its dimensions well. He can still picture his family in his head. He hears their movement, their individual breaths, and it is Danny who hears the dog first, whimpering in the kitchen, struggling to breathe, gasping, retching, and finally dying. He doesn't say a word. Danny suspects that his father hears the dying dog too, but can't or won't put the picture together for Joleen when she asks, "What's that noise, Daddy?"

"Nothing," Jim says. "It's nothing you kids need to know about."

A Legacy of Holes

AS WE DROVE across Kansas from Lawrence to visit the remnants of Greensburg, Dad told me he never thought the TV would mean so much. He said that when he was growing up in the early days of TV and people gathered nightly, ritualistically, in front of the screen as one or two regular shows would rise up from the fuzz, he still never imagined that television would have the influence it does now.

My generation is really the first generation to have television memories that are not mostly tinged with nostalgic, warm, and fuzzy undertones. We're perhaps the first generation to be raised by the TV as a substitute entertainer and authority, a major familial and cultural institution in our lives—with all the complicated dynamics that entails.

My dad spent most of his childhood outdoors, and he doesn't have any real memories of television shows or of much time spent in front of the tube. Instead, he's told me for years how he dug an underground fort in his backyard. He'd claim that it had a roof and a tunnel that stretched over to another part of the yard.

Whenever I've asked him why he built the fort, he never has a good answer. Usually he just chalks it up to boredom. I of course want to believe that it's more than that. Dad grew up during the first decades of the Cold War in a small farm town, not far from several large natural gas pumping stations and railroad lines.

"Targets," he admitted after I pressed him a bit more, "all of them. They told us the Russians had a missile pointed at us."

He also grew up not far from Holcomb, Kansas, where the Clutter family had been slaughtered by Perry Smith and Dick Hickok, and where Truman Capote wrote his seminal work of novelized fact, *In Cold Blood*, and where the black-and-white movie about the crime and the loss of innocence it represented was relived and re-created, then released to the public on December 14, 1967, during my dad's senior year in high school.

"Those killings and the book and even the movie changed the world for me," he said. "People started locking their doors after that. Everybody was afraid of everybody."

Dad doesn't credit fear for his hole, though. It was just something to do, something to keep himself busy. I had a hard time believing this. I still do on some level. Like many of his stories, it seems too detailed and odd to be a lie, and too fantastic to be true.

On our trip back to Greensburg after the May 4 tornado, I stood with him in the driveway of the house where he grew up, the house where my grandparents had lived for almost seventy years, as he pointed at the muddy, debris-filled corner of the small yard, to a scraggly patch of dirt next to the alley, fringed by the bedraggled remnants of a hedge.

"Right there," he said.

"What do you mean?" I asked.

"Me and Keith Kenyon, we dug that cave in the yard right there."

"But why?"

"I'm not sure. Nothing else to do, I guess."

Dad told me that they just started digging a hole one day. Just two boys with shovels. It began as a foxhole, a defensive position for some extended skirmish in a rock-throwing battle with the neighbor boy who lived on the other side of the hedge. That's how it started. But for whatever reason, Dad and Keith just kept digging and digging, and the hole grew deeper and deeper. A defensive position, he said.

I didn't ask him how long the battle lasted.

My father had a reputation for his barely bottled energy, as if he was born too big for the little farm town in Southwest Kansas; he was a ten-pound chunk of baby when he arrived, and he never stopped growing or moving. I'd heard a story or two about my grandmother trying to rein him in by tying him to the clothesline in the backyard. Dad once climbed a tree in the yard and fell out, bruising his arm badly. When his father came home and asked what had happened, Dad climbed back up the tree to show him and promptly fell out again. That time he broke his arm.

He claims, without any whiff of fabrication, that he kept and fed for some time (until it got too big and scary) a pet raccoon, and he will relate stories of riding his bike around the streets of Greensburg with his .22 rifle held across the handlebars. This was the '50s, small-town

Kansas, before the Clutter killings immortalized by Capote, before Vietnam—a time and place that had always, for so many reasons, seemed light years away from the world in which I lived but which had also seemed to be preserved in some small way in Greensburg.

It was exactly the sort of place the writers and producers of *The Day After* imagined Lawrence to be. Greensburg *was* the image of quiet, simple innocence, hard work, and pragmatism. It was a tangible, living touchstone for me not just to my father's past, but also to a past identity of Kansas and perhaps even our country. Now it was gone. Obliterated by wind.

DESPITE OUR DIFFERENT childhoods, there is at least one thing Dad and I shared that would forever shape our understanding of our place in the world—fear of the atomic bomb—and it would be the evolution of this fear and our response to it that often defined the difference between our generations.

Dad remembers how they told him in school that his hometown, Greensburg, was a prime target for the Russian missiles because of the web of natural gas pipelines and the massive booster station northwest of town, not to mention the railroad lines and the crops the Reds would try to poison, and of course the missile silos in Eastern Colorado and other Department of Defense installations, or secret bunkers that nobody knew about except for the government and the Reds.

These are, not surprisingly, many of the same reasons I was given for why Lawrence would be targeted by Soviet warheads in the '80s. One difference between Dad and me may be the way we absorbed this kind of information, this feeling of being targeted, and how it blended with what we knew and what we believed.

THAT DAY, FIFTY years ago, my grandmother must have emerged from the house, watched the boys hefting shovels of dirt, and believed it was better than the alternatives—most of which involved some kind of property destruction or bodily harm.

Soon enough the hole in the yard was so deep they had to climb in and out with a ladder and could stand upright without seeing over the edge. My grandmother must have been lost in a book or a painting or a TV show. Or maybe she just didn't care. This was the same woman who used to take my dad out on country roads in each new car they bought and tell him, "Let's see what this thing can do," before she slammed the pedal to the floor and tried to top out the speedometer. She had a wild side.

It's hard to say how the decision was made, but soon Dad and Keith were digging a tunnel too. Just wide enough for their bodies, the tunnel stretched from the floor of the hole up to the surface of the yard several feet away. The boys filched some lumber from the garage and covered the top of the hole, then spread dirt over the boards, concealing the hole.

It took some work, but before long they had a secret cave in the backyard. They grabbed a couple of flashlights and crawled down the tunnel into their own private hole. The boys sat there, sheltered from attack, and must have felt safe and secure, protected from the surface. I like to imagine my father there, huddled beneath the surface, dirt and dust filtering down into his hair, the dim glow of his flashlight just barely illuminating his smile.

I TOO USED to dream of living beneath the surface of the earth in my own underground house. Skylights and everything. Lots of white cabinets and walls and my very own bunker, a sort of inner sanctum. Twelve feet by twelve feet with twelve-inch concrete-block walls, steel-plated, insulated, air-conditioned, with its own generator and water system. Floor vaults packed to the gills with canned food and MREs. Frantic digging seemed like a perfectly appropriate response to fear of the apocalypse. I had it all planned out. Sketches, drawings, maps, and stories. Solar-powered. Well water. Light tubes. Somewhere alone in the woods, living off roots and berries and high-protein mush. I idealized the hermit life, the solitary male existence immortalized in books like *My Side of the Mountain* and, more recently, *Desert Solitaire* and *Into the Wild*. And of course I once tried to dig my own hole in the backyard. I didn't make it far before I quit. It was too much work and it was a lot more fun to just imagine my hole.

I'm sure I'm making too much of this legacy of holes, but is it a coincidence that I would later twice work as a tour guide for massive holes in the earth? At my first job working at a hole, I donned a hard hat and coveralls and led people 1,000 feet into the side of a mountain to tour an abandoned gold mine. I spent much of my day in near darkness.

At the second job, I worked as a tour guide at the Meteor Crater in the Northern Arizona desert, the site of a cataclysmic impact 50,000 years ago between an iron meteor and the earth, an impact that would have devastated all life for hundreds of miles in all directions. I used to tell stories about the effects of the impact, talk about TNT and shock waves, but never I mentioned its man-made analogues, Fat Man and Little Boy and others made just across the state line and up in the high mesas near Los Alamos, New Mexico.

I never told them how Flagstaff would have been reduced to rubble, but I did mention often that an impact on the magnitude of the impact that created Meteor Crater—one that would have sent a cloud of dust into the atmosphere that blocked out the sun—occurs about every 50,000 years.

"In other words," I used to say, "we're due for another one any day now."

Then I would ask for questions.

THOUGH I DOUBT he would make so much of his hole in the ground, I like to think my dad dug his hole for complicated reasons. My grandparents had a basement, which they could conceal with a hidden entrance in the dining room floor—a thick panel that folded up and locked into place to allow access to the stairs.

When it was time for dinner we always had to make sure that everyone was upstairs before we closed the entrance, covered it with carpet patches, and pulled the table out to make room for everyone. In case of a nuclear attack, my dad and his family would have sealed themselves in the basement until the bombs were done dropping. My grandmother's sewing room had small yellow-and-black signs above the door that read Fallout Shelter, and I can picture them all huddled in there together, surrounded by bolts of fabric, sewing machines, coffee cans, and plastic bins full of buttons.

They never built a traditional backyard bomb shelter, never installed the prefab kind mass-marketed in the '50s and sold to many of their neighbors. As we cruised the decimated blocks of Greensburg, I spotted several newer green plastic models rising out of the soil, looking like exposed septic tanks or artificial turtles. Perhaps my grandparents were holding out against the atomic paranoia or simply refusing to acknowledge the threat. Perhaps they were too cheap or too practical.

Perhaps my grandfather, a very wise man, understood the truth that my generation would understand well some thirty years later.

You had to come out of the shelter someday. Then what?

Dad can recall films in school, the ones with the cartoon turtle instructing them to duck and cover. He drilled with all the other kids, hiding under his desk, imagining the bombs dropping from the sky, and he had to know that there was no backyard shelter waiting for him at home, nothing to ensure *his* survival.

Maybe it's my own dramatic sense of personal history, but I think Dad dug his hole for more than fun. I think he felt some version of the fear that I felt as a child.

THE TOWN OF Greensburg's most recognizable and highly advertised landmark before the tornado was the Big Well. Billed as the "world's largest hand-dug well," the Big Well boasted a large silver water tower that stretched up into the sky, competing only with nearby grain silos for attention. It was topped with a green roof and had the words Big Well in black block letters spray-painted around its midriff. A gift store at the water tower's base sold postcards, painted plates, T-shirts, and other assorted kitsch; out front, beneath a metal cover with smudged viewing glass, sat the Big Well itself.

At 109 feet deep and thirty-two feet across, it was an impressive feat of human effort and engineering. To imagine men digging this well took leaps and bounds, and during my summer visits to Granddad and Grandma's house I regularly visited the Big Well gift shop and surrounding park. About once a year I paid my money and climbed the metal staircase down into the Big Well. There wasn't much to it. No guided tour. No stories of men dying in the well, being buried in the walls—just some placards with the history of the Big Well, the estimated amount of dirt removed, facts, numbers, that sort of thing. There was usually nobody else down there with me, and it was always cool and moist at the bottom. Goldfish swam in the murky water and moss grew on the stone walls. I liked it down there beneath the surface.

The May 4 F5 crumpled the legs of the water tower, toppled it over, and flattened the gift shop down to a knee-high pile of rubble of shattered souvenir plates and wet piles of postcard pulp. The Big Well itself, by the time I saw it, had been caged with cyclone fencing, its cover still intact but shrouded with a fading blue tarp. It looked like a large boxy casket.

I stood there, my fingers hooked through the fence, and wondered what it might have been like to wait out the storm in the Big Well, to look up and watch it pass over. I wondered about the sound. Would the storm's howl penetrate, bounce around in the well, and reach your ears? Or would it die in the cool space above? Would you have to dodge showers of broken glass? Perhaps you'd only see a silent rush of wind, rain, and debris passing before the lens-like opening of the hole above—as if you were watching the storm through a telescope, as if you were there but not there.

Sunday School

Iт was a Sunday in the summer of 1982 and I stood on the front porch of the Big Brick Church downtown. Mom adjusted my red clip-on tie. Clouds churned in the sky overhead and wind scattered leaves down the street, and with the big gusts the noise became a roar, like a crowd cheering for a show. Inside, I knew what awaited me—the cavernous sanctuary, the oppressive human silence, and the pasty soft voice of Pastor C.

"You look so nice today," Mom said.

"Nu-uh," Matt said. "He looks dumb."

"Shut up," I said.

"Boys!" Mom said. "That's enough. Let's just go inside. The youth sermon will be starting soon. The pastor will be waiting."

Looking back, I can see that Pastor C. was no Rev. Fisher. Aside from his lack of dramatic flair, he pronounced donkey "dunkey"—as in "Jesus rode into Bethlehem on a *dunkey*."

This always bothered me.

He also wore this colorful Guatemalan sash over his black robe, but as far as I could tell he'd never actually been to Guatemala, and I think he wore the sash to look multicultural or tolerant or something. I thought he just looked sort of silly.

Pastor C. never talked about a city "shorn of its beauty," not a word about "sack-cloth and ashes." He talked about his missionary work in Hawaii as if he'd been stationed in a faraway land. But he did also talk a lot about peace and love and—as much as he could—tried to speak out against the nuclear arms race and the Cold War. It was hard to get too political as the youth minister.

When I was eight or nine, I appreciated any kind of anti-nuke stance from a religious authority—even if he wasn't really much of an authority. Pastor C. was an assistant pastor—the youth minis-ter—at the Big Brick Church downtown where Mom worked as his administrative assistant. He was still sucking up to a man I'll call Pastor A., the senior pastor and a fiery orator who somehow made our milquetoast form of Protestantism feel downright evangelical. Nobody could hold a candle to Pastor A. He yelled and screamed and swayed his body around and got all red-faced for the Lord.

Sometimes you'd swear he was going to explode.

Pastor C., on the other hand, was known for his even tones and measured pitch. He had a methodical, librarian-like delivery of the Word. If Pastor A. was a lightning bolt for the Lord, then Pastor C. was a dripping faucet for the Lord—half hypnotic, half annoying. His specialty was these short, pithy youth sermons that always ended in some cliché moral lesson from the Bible, a practical tip for our everyday lives.

After a couple of songs and a short prayer from Pastor A., Pastor C. would raise his arms up, palms upturned, calling all the children down to sit on the altar steps with him. When he moved he made these sweeping motions with his arms—gathering up his thick robes and controlling the cord of his microphone—that made him look like he was floating just above the ground, paddling the air like a pious ghost.

With all of us kids gathered around, he'd tie knots in a rope, fill glasses with water, break loaves of bread, and tell us a story about his visit to the supermarket or an old folks' home or a particularly cute question his daughter asked him when he was putting her to bed. Most of the sermons sounded the same and he often asked for volunteers—which explains why I usually lurked in the back, hiding behind other, more eager and pious, children.

Pastor C. made me sleepy and a little nauseous. His voice was like a warm glass of milk, and I was lactose-intolerant. He had a way about him that always seemed sort of slippery and soft to me. I wasn't a true believer. I didn't trust his authority.

At that age, I would've definitely done better with some kind of apocalyptic fire-and-brimstone preacher—someone even more extreme than Pastor A., someone more like the good Reverend Fisher and his sack-cloth and ashes, someone who might castigate us for our sins, blaming the impending apocalypse on adultery and thievery, or just on Missouri, maybe play rock guitar from the pulpit and drink strychnine, someone who could stand up to the apocalypse, rather than kowtowing and capitulating to politicians and pop culture.

Sure, his stories would've been just as predictable as Pastor C.'s little life lessons of love and kindness, but at least they'd be full of wrath and pestilence. They'd smite you. At least he might have busted out some screaming guitar licks for Jesus or spoken in tongues or swilled death from a Mason jar.

After Pastor C.'s sermon, the children were excused for Sunday school, and this was really what we were all waiting for. This is why we sat through his stories and lessons.

We were rewarded with two things: the blood and the body of Christ. Or, in our case, fruit punch and Danish butter cookies (the kind that come packed in a big round tin with a country windmill on the lid)—clear evidence of our slippery liberal ways. We didn't kneel before the black robes to take our sacrament. We sat at tiny tables covered with construction paper and cookie crumbs, and some of us wondered about the windmill on the cookie tin's lid more than we did about Jesus.

To me, fruit punch and Danish butter cookies were the epitome of religion, faith, and church. As far as I was concerned, the ritual consumption of butter cookies made all the hymns and psalms and organ music tolerable. Even at an early age, my lips stained with red punch, I thought religion—at least Pastor C.'s version of religion—was way too benign, insignificant, and completely inadequate for answering the larger questions I had about the world.

ALONG WITH ATTENDING church regularly, I was also dutifully marching through the Boy Scout ranks (just as my father marched when he was a boy), with every intention of becoming an Eagle Scout. This seemed like a sure road to survival, a guarantee. *The Official Boy Scout Handbook* promised as much. I loved that book. It came with practical lessons, pictures, charts, and loads of important-sounding facts about fire-building, knot-tying, and other crucial skills. If the apocalypse came, I imagined myself holding not a Bible but *The Official Boy Scout Handbook* clutched in my fingers, hoisted aloft against the rapture—a talisman, the true Word as it were.

Be gone, foul demons! For I am Boy Scout, Man-Child, a Servant of the Light!

I also just liked the Scout fashion sense. I collected rows of embroidered merit badges and patches on my army-green shoulder sash. I set records at summer camp for badges earned. I was unstoppable and quickly surpassed the number of merit badges my father earned during his time in the Scouts. When I ribbed him about it, he made excuses about growing up in Western Kansas and not having the same opportunities I did. Matt, along with some other ambitious kids in the troop, earned a lot of merit badges, but few, if any of us, possessed the God and Country badge.

My dad, the same man who regularly begged out of church services at the Big Brick Church by saying "I did my time," told me that the God and Country badge was one he earned as a boy, worked hard for, and the one of which he was most proud.

"This one is different," he said. "Not just anyone has the God and Country."

I shrugged off his subtle dig at my plethora of badges as he explained that this badge was distinct from the others, more serious, more important than Basketry or Swimming or Archery. It strikes me only now how ridiculously and optimistically patriotic this badge was. Back then, it took only a little convincing before I eventually decided to pursue it. Mom arranged for me to meet with Pastor C. from the Big Brick Church. He would be my teacher, my guide in the journey to a deeper relationship with God and my country.

This worried me right off the bat.

I met with Pastor C. in the evenings for my lessons, after school and dinner, when the big old church was all dark and scary and you could hear bats fluttering in the hallways. They lived in the belfry or the attic or something, and they only came out at night, cruising the hallways for bugs.

Mom drove me there and worked downstairs in her office while I received instruction from Pastor C. We met in an upstairs classroom in a newer addition to the church with the fluorescent lights bright and buzzing overhead. It didn't feel right to me. Maybe because he wasn't wearing his robes and his Guatemalan sash, but a suit instead, with a collared shirt and a cross-shaped lapel pin on his jacket. He had hair like a furniture salesman and a voice like a filmstrip narrator.

"So, Steve. What do you think 'God and country' means?" he asked me. "What do you want this merit badge to be about?"

I didn't have any idea. God to me was mostly a character in a story. I was much more interested in the things that people did in the name of God—people like John Brown, or even Quantrill. Maybe those men who'd blown up the marines or shot down that airplane. But I didn't really feel like I could say these things to Pastor C. I guess I wanted him to tell *me* what it meant. I wanted him to make sense of God and country and war, maybe with one of his happy little sermons—but I think I also knew that religion felt so far removed from the Cold War, and specifically from the brutal science of nuclear immolation, that it seemed painfully incapable of responding to the reality of life in the '80s.

Though I couldn't have said it at the time, I think I was beginning to understand then that nuclear war was, for me, pretty strong evidence that God did not exist—or at least not the sort of omnipotent, benevolent mutant God I needed.

I didn't say any of this. Instead I tried to find a way to get Pastor C. to say "*dunkey*."

"What kind of animal was it again that Jesus rode into town after he rose from the dead? A horse?"

Silence.

"Tell me, Steve," Pastor C. said, smoothing his hands over his knee, "how *are* things at home?"

Pastor C. and I never seemed to get anywhere with this God-and-country stuff. God and country. God and *dunkey*. We never had any major breakthroughs. No revelations. No commitment to patriotism or peace. There were a couple of boring discussions about the Christian underpinnings of the U.S. Constitution and the importance of faith to our Founding Fathers. But I knew most of this already, and I didn't feel like I could talk to him about nuclear war or my fears of dying from radiation sickness, or of burning in a fire. I couldn't share my dreams of genetic mutation. He clearly didn't want to hear a detailed rundown of the events leading up to Lincoln's assassination, and I didn't trust him enough to admit that as much as I loved *The Incredible Hulk*, Lou Ferrigno gave me horrible nightmares.

There was a superficiality to our discussions about everything, including God and country, and I began to doubt if I even wanted the merit badge. It felt like he just sat there staring at me, breathing through his nose and writing things on a yellow legal pad. Eventually I convinced my parents to let me stop meeting with Pastor C. Things weren't easy at home and they didn't fight me much on the decision.

I confess. I cut and run from my God and Country merit badge.

I had no idea then why parents pushed me into it in the first place, or why Pastor C. might be concerned about me, so overly worried and just plain weird. I had no idea why he asked questions about my parents and my life at home. That didn't seem like part of the lesson plan on God and country.

THE '80S SEEMED to be filled with confusing lessons. Television, like Sunday school, was just another window—though some days it felt like a funhouse mirror. One day during the filming of *The Day After*, my little brother and I returned to the Big Brick Church with Mom and found something we never expected.

A large tractor-trailer sat out in front, taking up the parking spaces we normally used. As we approached it from around the side of the church, I noticed that its back doors were open and a ramp led up into the cargo area. Inside, I saw what appeared to be a menagerie of animals. Or fake animals—it was kind of hard to tell the difference, even up close.

"Oh, boys, wait," Mom said when she saw us approach the truck cautiously. "No, don't."

But it was too late. We saw them.

A large brown and white cow, bloated and dusty with ash, stood in the trailer with its tongue hanging out. Another nearly identical cow stood beside the first, its hide covered with crusty radiation sores. There was a white horse, the Dahlberg dog, a cat or two, a couple of goats, a shelf with some pigeons, and a few stuffed songbirds. Obviously we had stumbled across some kind of prop truck for the film.

"Did those cows used to be real?" my brother asked.

Mom said, "Yes, I suppose they were real at some point, but not anymore. Now they're stuffed and the producers are using them for the movie."

Mom ushered us away from the truck, pushing us back toward the church. She had to work and we had to come with her. We had to forget about that stuff, she said. It's not important, she said. Just fake dead things. That's all. Push the images out of your head. You don't need to see that stuff. She told us to forget about it . . . and I did. Completely. Every last detail invented, re-created from my mom's story of that day, the imagined carnage taking the place of real memory. Some days I'm afraid to ask her what else I missed, what might have been happening offscreen, in the margins of the story.

DAHLBERG VARIATION

Helen Oaks doesn't like her car, the Cadillac. Her husband, the good Doctor Oaks, bought it for her fiftieth birthday, and she always felt it was too big. Now she has proof. Damn boat of a car, she thinks.

She leans up against the front quarter-panel and sets her purse on the hood. Who needs a Cadillac in Kansas City? And here she is, stuck in the Oak Park Mall parking lot, the front end of the Caddie smashed up, and this poor woman in the other car bawling like a cow. She'll be late. That much is certain now. She'll be late for her meeting at the church with Pastor Dean. He'll worry about her. Or at least she imagines that he worries about her, that he thinks of her often, at times when he shouldn't.

Helen picks up her purse. She will tell her husband all about this when he gets home later today. She'll tell him that he can drive the damn Cadillac to the hospital in Lawrence tomorrow. She'll drive the Toyota. How long can it take to get a police officer here? She called twenty minutes ago. The blond woman in the Chevy is just sitting behind the wheel, shaking her head, crying. Helen thinks her car looks too big for her as well, the poor woman. She hopes the woman isn't hurt or something as she strolls over to her window.

"Ma'am?" she asks. "Are you OK? You're not hurt, are you?"

Eve Dahlberg turns to her, gazing up at her face. "No, no. I'm OK."

"I'm really sorry," Helen says, "I mean, it's just a fender bender. It'll be all right. It's these cars, honey. That's what I think. They're too damn big. I told my husband that I didn't want a car that big, that it was a waste with what gasoline costs these days and the energy crisis."

"Yes, you're right," Eve says. "That's true what you said. I don't really like to drive. I should have stayed home."

"You sure you're OK?" Helen asks. "The police will be here soon. We have to report it."

"Oh, I know. I'm fine. It's just that . . . Oh, never mind." Eve whimpers and sputters, tears welling up in her eyes.

"What is it?" Helen leans in close to the car. "Is it your husband? Is something wrong?"

"Yes," Eve chokes out before bursting into a flood of tears. "I just wanted to have the wedding. We've been planning it for so long." She thinks of Denise's dress, the delicate veil, the long train of silk.

"What is it, honey? You can tell me. Will your husband hurt you? I understand these things. Just tell him it's my fault, OK? It was all my fault."

Eve looks up at her. "What?" She doesn't understand.

"Your husband." Helen pauses. "I thought maybe he would hurt you or something. You know. Because of the car." She pointed at the rear of Eve's car, the dented bumper.

"No. Oh, God! No. That's not it. No." Eve shakes her head, touches it to the steering wheel. "My daughter. She's supposed to be married tomorrow. She's my oldest. Jim was so proud."

Helen pauses for moment. "That's just wonderful," she says, thinking of her own daughter and her plans to run off to Boston to be with a man. She worries about her, that's all. She just wants what's best for her daughter. "You want to get out of the car, maybe get some air?" Helen asks, and Eve climbs out of her car, into the sun.

The two women lean up against the Chevy at the edge of the mall's parking lot. It's hot and bright and all around them they hear police sirens screaming. Something's happening. Something bad.

"It's taking forever to get an officer here," Helen says, straightening her skirt. "What's your name?" she asks.

"Eve," the woman says. "Eve Dahlberg," She cups her hands to her face and lets out a couple of high-pitched sobs.

"Helen Oaks," Helen says, extending her hand politely. Eve grips her hand firmly and jerks her arm like it's a well pump. Helen looks at the woman's wide denim skirt and twill plaid shirt and figures she lives outside of town, somewhere on a farm between here and Lawrence, maybe down south near Harrisonville. She's seen women like this at the mall before. They always look out of place.

"It's OK, honey," Helen says as she pats the woman on the shoulder. "You'll make the wedding tomorrow."

Eve looks up at her, making eye contact for the first time. "There's not going to be a wedding tomorrow. There's not going to be anything tomorrow."

"Oh, let's not be melodramatic," Helen says. "It's just a fender bender."

"Don't you know what's happening? Don't you realize that there's going to be a war, a nuclear war?" Eve stands up straight, turns to face Helen, and grabs her by the shoulders. Helen recoils and tries to pull away but can't break the grip. Eve shouts in her face, "We're all going to die!"

Helen squirms away and stumbles back toward her car.

"I'm sorry. I have to go," Eve hollers as she climbs into her dented Chevy, cranks the engine over, and speeds off, her tires squealing on the pavement.

Helen climbs back into her Cadillac. It's hot and stuffy like an oven. She's miles from home now. She starts the engine and turns on the air conditioner. Cars stream out of the mall's parking lot. People are running now, streaming out of the doors. They seem to be in some kind of panic. Mothers clutch their children's hands and run. Some of them are crying too.

Her daughter hates her. Helen knows this for sure. She knows that nobody will come for her now. A thin bead of sweat forms at her hairline and slides down her forehead. Helen blots at it with her shirtsleeve, leaving a pink makeup stain on her cuff.

She will just stay here. She will wait for the police. Helen reaches for the radio, touches the knob, then pulls her hand away. She doesn't want to hear the news; she just wants to pretend that none of it matters, that her husband will come home early from Lawrence, forget about work, and the two of them will talk or not talk about their days and their daughter. Helen wants to pretend that there isn't another woman—a nurse, probably—and that their marriage is as strong as ever.

Helen raises her hand, trying to hold it perfectly still like her husband does when he's showing off his "surgeon hands." She looks at her wrist and realizes she left her watch sitting on the counter at home. She tries to keep her hand still. It trembles and quivers and, for the first time in a long time, Helen is afraid for her family and her future. Just as several police cars pull into the mall parking lot, she slumps over on the long vinyl seat, curls up, rolls down, and disappears beneath the dashboard.

Yellow Warning Notes

Things were tense around the house in the early '80s and it had little to do with foreign policy or flying monkeys. The trouble was all domestic relations. Mom seemed distant and Dad acted just plain angry at the world. My younger brother was characteristically oblivious or simply too stubborn to admit that his family had failed him. After our brief stint in the duplex, we'd all moved into the house on Stratford Road, right near Hillcrest Elementary School, and I chose a room in the basement as my own. I'd wanted some independence and separation from the rest of the family and liked having my room down there. I liked the darkness, the quiet, the solitude. I liked the safety of being underground. But it wasn't always an easy place to live.

We had mice. Lots of them.

At night I heard them scurry-skitter across the ceiling tiles over my bed, making frantic, hair-tickling noises as they moved about. There seemed to be dozens of them, and, occasionally, something much larger than a mouse galumphed across the ceiling, nearly, it seemed, falling through and onto my bed. A rat? A possum? A squirrel? I wasn't sure and I didn't really want to know.

I banged on the walls with my fists, but the mice didn't care. They were always running, always clawing. Driving me crazy. One day, after I complained enough, Dad pulled down a ceiling tile and set a trap with peanut butter. We caught seven mice that day. He pulled each one out of the trap and, if it was still alive, let the dog maul its broken body for a while before tossing it in the trash.

When it rained really hard in the spring and early summer, the basement window wells filled with water and leaked. One morning I climbed out of bed into an inch of water on the floor. The worst part of living in the basement, though, wasn't the flooding, but my fear of fire. I'd seen the public service announcements on television and the numerous educational filmstrips and programs at school about the danger of house fires—especially to children. I was haunted by the ubiquitous images of mothers standing on the sidewalk, screaming "My baby! My baby!" as the house burst into flames and collapsed into cinders and dust. I always wondered how it was that all the adults always made it out of the house. Families were encouraged to hold fire drills and practice escape routes. This seemed easy enough for my parents and my brother. They lived upstairs and were surrounded by large windows and doors. I lived in the basement, and at the top of the stairs, my only exit, sat a massive '60s-era Kenmore oven—a fireball waiting to happen. At the bottom of the stairs, the prehistoric furnace lurked and clanked and rumbled with flame. The water heater was down there too, hissing with blue gas, threatening to blow shrapnel. My only exit was completely cut off by potential flame-throwing devices.

Replacing my dreams of the Incredible Hulk were vivid and terrifying nightmares of being trapped in a house fire, burning to death as the house collapsed around me—like those children I'd seen in the filmstrips at school. The fear was always about being trapped with no escape.

Before long, I spent most nights sleeping on the couch upstairs in the living room, faced with a huge bank of bay windows that I figured I could crash through easily if a fire broke out. It got to the point where I couldn't spend the night in my own room. The fire dreams were just too much. One day, out of the blue, Mom and Dad announced they had an idea they thought I might like. They brought me upstairs and into the small office space on the main floor between their room and Matt's room. Dad had a sly grin on his face and I knew he was up to something. He opened the closet and pointed at the floor. "You know what's under that floor?" he asked me.

"Nope," I said.

"Your bedroom," Mom said.

"Huh?" I said, realizing slowly that they meant the closet was located directly over one corner of my basement bedroom and if we were to, say, cut a hole in the floor, we could look down into my bedroom. To their credit, Mom and Dad waited for me to understand. They waited for eye contact, recognition.

Then Dad said, "I say we build a trapdoor and put in a ladder so you have an escape route in case of a fire. You'd have your own secret entrance." He let the idea sit for a while, hovering in the space between us. I loved it. I wanted to let it float for a few minutes and appreciate the loft and weight.

"Cool," I said, and Mom hugged me, knowing what this meant.

Later that day, Dad brought his power tools into the house, ripped up the carpet in the closet, and after drilling some pilot holes, sawed a huge chunk out of the hardwood floor. He didn't even think twice about it, didn't balk at the idea of cutting a gaping chasm in the house. He installed a rope ladder and a trap door that allowed me to climb onto my chest of drawers and up the ladder into the coat closet upstairs.

Somehow—even with all the other crap in their lives, all the obvious distance between them—Mom and Dad knew that I would love the idea of my own secret escape hatch, my own private Batman-like entrance. Maybe they understood me after all. There was little I wanted more in the world than some kind of hidden passageway, a secret doorway or room of some kind, and they'd given it to me. Just when I thought I was on my own with this whole fear-of-fire business, Mom and Dad stepped up to save me. They also gave me a release from my nightmares, a door back to my own space. My dreams settled down after a few days and the comfort of my secret escape let me sleep again—finally.

More than once I climbed up on my dresser, popped the hatch open, pulled down the rope ladder, and hoisted myself out—just to practice for the inevitable fire. Survival, I understood, takes careful planning. Survival was about believing you could escape—even if the reality departed from the truth somewhere between the basement and the surface.

IT WAS RIGHT around this time that Dad brought Post-it Notes home from the office. They were a new thing back then, and I thought they were fantastic, nearly revolutionary. Notes with sticky stuff. Notes you could stick to things or people. Notes you could "post" indiscriminately. And without the hassle of tape!

I found endless joy in sticking yellow pieces of paper to my brother that said *Kick me* and *I'm stupid*, and affixing notes to myself that said *I'm with stupid* with an arrow pointing to my brother. I'd been at this for a while one day—sticking Post-it Notes to the dog, the furniture, and anything else I could reach—when Dad came home from work.

I could see right away that things weren't good between Mom and him. They avoided each other, barely spoke to each other, ignored me completely, and lobbed looks over my head, across the room. The posturing had begun again and I was just tired of it. I felt like a beleaguered ambassador from the Land of Children.

I wrote the words *Kiss me* on a yellow Post-it Note and stuck it to my mom.

I wrote *Hug me* on another one and stuck it to my dad.

Then I pushed them toward each other. It was like shoving two continents. Their tectonic plates grinded and squealed and heaved in revolt. But my push was volcanic. Tired of the incessant boiling, I wanted an eruption.

I wanted parental Pangaea.

They moved closer, angling away, until I caught them and forced a confrontation. They stood there in front of each other, staring at the yellow Post-it Notes as if they were written in a foreign language.

"Not now, Steven," Mom said, and her eyes watered up. She pulled her note off, turned away, and fled to another room.

Dad peeled his note off, handed it to me, and drifted like a landmass through the kitchen, out into the living room, then sank into a chair.

This is when I knew it was over.

Later, my parents came to find me in my room and asked why I was crying.

"You're getting a divorce, aren't you?" I asked.

They were stunned. They had nothing to say except, "Yes. Yes, we are."

"I knew it," I said.

"How?" they asked.

"I just knew it," I said. "I've felt it coming."

"We're so sorry, Steven," Mom said, her face flushed with blood, red as a flag.

"Why?" I asked, though I didn't really expect an answer.

"Your mother has decided to leave," he said and looked at Mom. She slumped against the wall and I thought she might collapse.

"What?"

"Your mother has . . . " Dad was crying now.

"We just don't love each other any longer," Mom interrupted, her eyes settling on my father.

I looked up at her.

"It's true," she mumbled. "I'm so sorry."

Right then the wall came tumbling down for good. The long Cold War was over. The end arrived that quickly and quietly and bloodlessly, and the silent wash of that moment still hangs with me.

Boom, gone.

Our family—or at least my image of our family—was devastated in an instant, reduced to shards. And I knew I'd have to step out of the ruins, push through to the other side, and find a way to adapt.

The Four Horsemen

6.

1.

ON SEPTEMBER 1, 1983, Korean Air Lines Flight 007 lifted off from Anchorage, Alaska, bound for Seoul, South Korea. The flight originated in New York and the plane had the words I ♥ New York emblazoned on the fuselage. The flight was to follow a precarious course, just skirting the edge of Soviet airspace before reaching its destination. At some point, the plane drifted over an invisible line, and it would never return.

When I heard the news, it wasn't too difficult to imagine my face pressed to the plastic window of the airplane, everyone around me asleep, drifting into dreamland as we sailed over continents and oceans. Did I see the Su-15 fighter, the Soviet interceptor? No. I saw nothing but what I imagined. Escorts perhaps. Air greeters. The welcoming. A shadow of threat. Clouds slipping past by like smoke. This was just a vacation, a trip home, a mission. Something right became suddenly so wrong. Were those red tracer rounds zipping past?

Perhaps there were other kids on the flight collecting bits of swag and detritus—tickets, barf bags, menus, maps, and boarding passes— to paste in their vacation scrapbook. I hoped for them that they felt nothing, that death came quickly.

The passengers knew nothing of the warnings, the straying of the aircraft over invisible lines of airspace. When I heard of "airspace," I imagined translucent walls of light rising into the air, marking boundaries of air space, hovering traffic signals identifying territory, red lights warning us to stop, slow, go. It seemed fantastical to think that a country could claim the air overhead as its property.

The missile ripped the plane open, spread the ribs of the fuselage, and battered hearts and bodies with concussive force. The plane lost pressure, lost altitude, lost. It dropped off the radar, into the Sea of

Japan, and sank to the bottom. There would be no emergency landing on a frozen lake, no survivors.

The plane's black boxes were taken by Soviet divers who must have ignored the crush of corpses still trapped inside, perhaps the carnage of cuttlefish feeding in the wreckage. The information was secreted away, protected, kept from family members for nine years. The gravesite of the passengers on KAL 007 was hidden from our government and from the victims' families, and because of the lack of information, the absence of closure, conspiracy theories persisted, suggesting that the plane had actually been forced to land like KAL 902 was five years earlier, the passengers taken prisoner and kept hidden in a Siberian prison.

Perhaps it's true that KAL Flight 007 took a similar course to U.S. spy planes that regularly tested the amorphous borders of airspace, and the Soviets, feeling threatened, had grown tired of intelligence incursions. Perhaps it's true that our own surveillance contributed to the tragedy. And perhaps it's just a sublime coincidence that the flight number of a plane accused of spying was 007—but these sorts of stories are full of sublime coincidences.

It was hard separate the truth of these events from the fiction. All I knew was that Reagan seemed to simultaneously grieve and revel in the tragedy, using it as fuel to feed the fire of anti-Soviet sentiment.

Reagan held up the tragedy of KAL 007 as yet another example of the threat posed by the Evil Empire, yet another item in a long list of reasons why it was important for the United States to win the nuclear arms race, and why it was important for us to trust his authority. He was very convincing.

2.

ON OCTOBER 23, 1983, one month before *The Day After* would air, reports surfaced from Beirut, Lebanon—a foreign place, far from home, from Kansas, a place I could barely imagine. Truck bomb. Terrorist. Two hundred forty-one U.S. military servicemen dead. I heard the news and tried to hear the lilting language, the call to prayer from mosques drifting over the city, tried to understand the alien landscape smelling of wood smoke and olive groves.

I could only place myself in the high-rise barracks, could only see myself as a soldier sitting at a small wooden desk, writing a letter home to his family. From the landscape of my imagination, the perch of my mind, I overlooked the front gate of the marine compound. I ran from this vision, from the truck bomb, its engine whining high—a sound a soldier would know as wrong, the noise racing toward him—the wide-eyed terrorist behind the wheel. I imagined further the sound of gates crashing, the shattering, the puncture of the thin film between safety and danger. I saw the slamming of the truck into the building and the pregnant pause filled with the birth of a blast blooming up from below.

I imagined the reality until I couldn't take it any longer, and then it was just the pictures I saw on the news: the pile of concrete and steel, the rebar poking out like harsh whiskers. I imagined the fall, the crater, the pit of my stomach, the last thing a marine might have felt, the last memory of his wife's smell, the soft spot on her neck, the sweet stink of her sweat.

Two hundred forty-one men died that day in October, and news spread fast, zooming out on airwaves, popping up in pictures. I imagined the sound of rescue dogs sniffing overhead, the scrape of boots, the *tap-tap-tap* sound of the search for survivors.

3.

ON OCTOBER 25, 1983, two days after the Beirut bombing of the marine barracks, U.S. troops invaded the island of Grenada. We rolled up like a tsunami of military force to suppress a small communist guerilla uprising that supposedly threatened a small cadre of American medical students.

This was the first war event of my active memory. Vietnam had ended before I was conscious of it. This was a new sort of war, justified by vague references to the threat of mysterious Communist guerrillas in the jungles of Grenada and Nicaragua, and potential for an invasion through our southern border. I'd never even heard of Grenada; but once again I turned to movies for answers.

Clint Eastwood films of the '70s and early '80s played a large part in my understanding of justice and morality. I'm not proud of this, necessarily, but I doubt I'm alone in my juvenile appreciation for Dirty Harry and similar sorts of characters and what they taught me about the world.

Despite my greatest hopes that the 1986 Eastwood-directed movie, *Heartbreak Ridge*, starring Eastwood himself and Mario Van Peebles, would provide clarification and guidance on the "war" in Grenada, a window into understanding the conflict and its justifications, it was sadly lacking in moral lessons, the sort of clear black-and-white answers to tough questions that Eastwood's characters were usually so accomplished at providing. In fact, it's rather difficult to say exactly what *Heartbreak Ridge* was all about, what the point of it was supposed to be, but the film was still nominated for an Academy Award that year.

Most of what I remember is Eastwood, playing decorated marine veteran Gunnery Sergeant Highway, "Gunny," chomping on a cigar and yelling at lazy recon recruits in a hoarse, gravelly voice, spewing out lots of coarse language and stereotypical things like "candy ass" and "pansies."

One soldier is played by the charming and curly-haired scamp Van Peebles. Another private, nicknamed "the Swede," is played by a mountain of a man whose other identity was as a lineman for the Kansas City Chiefs football team. There was the requisite smarmy major, a man with no combat experience who makes life unnecessarily difficult for Eastwood's character. Gunny doesn't need this shit, doesn't want it. He's a dinosaur, a Cold War relic.

Before he retires, Sergeant Highway is hoping for a final shot at combat, one last chance for military victory, and when the "war" breaks out in Grenada, in the context of the film, it seems not just convenient but almost as if it was manufactured specifically for Eastwood. As you might expect, Gunny rallies the ragtag group, motivates them to work together as a team, and the United States—by virtue of Eastwood's victory—once again stems the rising tide of communism.

4.

IN OCTOBER 1983, in the municipal courts of Douglas County, Kansas, through a series of filings, my parents' divorce was officially finalized and recorded.

7

Nuclear Summit

On the Sunday evening of November 21, 1983, *The Day After* was broadcast on ABC to an audience of 100 million viewers, garnering the second-highest Nielsen rating ever for a televised movie, outwatched only by *Gone with the Wind*.

In those few hours, Lawrence became a star—a glorious, dying star, the kind of supernova phenomenon most people see through a telescope. My family and I—everyone in town, really—all stood on the surface, waving at the viewers.

By that point, Mom had already moved out into a tiny two-bedroom apartment, but for the movie premiere we all reunited for a summit of sorts at my dad's house, down in the basement. All of us gathered to watch the drama.

Mom sat on one side, Dad on the other; my brother and I sat in between them. My parents figured it would be easier for us to experience the movie together, easier to pretend that we had the security of family to protect us from nuclear war. But it was cold in that basement, cold and quiet save for the noise of the television.

When the bombs dropped on-screen, I had to leave the room and hide in my closet. I waited there in the dark until Dad told me it was safe to come out. Later, back at her apartment, Mom would sit down on my bed and tell me that when she was a little girl, she had a space in her closet too, and, when things were especially bad at home, she would crawl inside and shut the door and pretend that she was in control of her own world and that everything was perfect.

One of my childhood friends sat with her family in front of the TV as CBS News cameras watched them watching the movie. For two hours the cameras watched them watching. Her father, a professor at the university, told me, "It was all very bizarre. I suppose they were hoping to capture an unfiltered reaction to the movie. They had these bright lights shining in our faces."

My wife, Rachel, remembers watching the movie with her best friend from down the street. Many people have memories of watching with their church youth group or with some safe number of people. Children were advised not to watch it alone. Many kids were simply forbidden by their parents from tuning in at all, the movie cast in the same taboo category as horror films and pornography.

60 Minutes did a story too, and Lawrence made the cover of numerous national magazines, including *Time* and *Newsweek*. Congressmen in both houses spoke out both for and against the movie, arguing that it was either anti-nuke propaganda or that it was an important, realistic wake-up call for America. Stories even circulated about Reagan watching the film and it causing something of a stir in the upper levels of the executive branch too. All of this for a TV movie.

DIRECTOR NICHOLAS MEYER worked with screenwriter Edward Hume to make *The Day After*. When commercial sponsors pulled support and Meyer himself threatened to quit unless he retained editorial control, ABC mercifully cut the film down from its original four-hour miniseries format to a two-hour feature presentation—guessing correctly that most Americans weren't likely to tune in night after night for a depressingly extended look at the days after a nuclear attack on our country.

In the midst of an unprecedented level of hype, ABC ran the movie as usual on a Sunday night, breaking occasionally for a word from their more courageous commercial sponsors, right up until the bombs dropped on-screen. After that, they ran the film without commercial interruption (or commercial sponsorship)—something that would be almost unthinkable today, especially on network television.

The film starred Steve Guttenberg, John Lithgow, JoBeth Williams, Amy Madigan, and John Cullum—all actors who, though well-established now, were relative unknowns at the time—and the cast was headlined by Jason Robards, one of several actors quoted as saying that they did the movie because they felt that it carried an important message.

A MONTH BEFORE the official network premiere and just a couple of days before the bombing of the marine barracks in Beirut, many Lawrence citizens previewed the movie with the mayor, David Longhurst, in the student union on campus—the same building firebombed during the Days of Rage in 1970.

The special advanced screening was followed by a massive candlelight vigil on the lawn beneath the university's World War II memorial bell tower. Mayor Longhurst was scheduled to address the crowd. With his friends and fellow citizens holding candles aloft, Longhurst admitted to me recently, he didn't know what to say, didn't know how to comfort them. He'd been to Vietnam. He'd seen bad things, and the movie still terrified him.

Longhurst recalled, "There was an absolute silence, and I was overwhelmed with the feeling that here were all these people who had just shared this devastating experience portrayed in the movie, and they were now all looking to me for words of hope, of reassurance . . . to tell them how everything was going to be OK."

Talk about some pressure.

The people of Lawrence made a blanket of light on the lawn below the stage. Each of them held a candle, and together they sang songs of peace. It looked very much like an antiwar protest from the '60s or '70s. Mayor Longhurst knew what he *should* say, knew he should talk about the eternal spirit of Lawrence and the hope for the future.

He recalled for them a scene in the movie where the little Dahlberg girl, Joleen, played by local girl Ellen Anthony, overhears news reports about escalating tensions between the U.S. and the Soviets. Joleen looks up at her father, Jim, and asks, "There isn't going to be a war, is there, Daddy?" But of course the war has already begun, and everyone but her seems to realize it. On the screen it's only a matter of minutes before the missiles arrive.

On the stage, Mayor Longhurst expressed his deep sense of despair and hopelessness, but, like a good leader must do, he turned it into something else—a trumpet to action, a message from the future, a wake-up call. He told the crowd that we must never allow this situation to occur, or, rather, we should always be able to answer such a question from our children—the question that Joleen posed to her father—with "No." We must be able to protect them from the kind of world depicted and predicted in *The Day After*.

Mayor Longhurst talked about peace and nuclear disarmament and how Reagan and Andropov should meet man to man, father to father, and talk, just *talk* about things. Then he invited the men to meet in Lawrence for a summit of sorts, a meeting of "two fathers," as he put it.

Later, his words would be reprinted in news stories all over the world. Both countries would, in fact, issue official statements in response to Mayor Longhurst's suggestion.

I liked the image of the two Cold War leaders seated on a bench in South Park, in downtown Lawrence, with the sounds of children playing in the background, perhaps the old train engine in the distance, and the history of Quantrill lingering in the hollows—the famous Lawrence summit of '83 that ended the nuclear arms race.

Because of his leadership in Lawrence, the mayor was invited to the Soviet Union to meet with Soviet officials. He'd gone to Washington with a group of children to meet with senators and state representatives. He'd shined in the spotlight, coming off as the eternally hopeful Midwestern mayor calling for Reagan and Andropov to meet as men and fathers, to just talk like friends. But then the newspapers and magazines and TV shows turned their attention somewhere else and he was just the mayor of Lawrence, a small targeted town in the small state of Kansas.

DAHLBERG VARIATION

Danny Dahlberg knows that his home has been targeted, but he is different from the other children. He sees things they don't. Perhaps he's had visions too. He wears Toughskin jeans too, the kind of pants with the imitation-leather patch stitched to the pocket and the white denim worn thin around the knees—not from praying, but from playing in the dust.

With two older sisters in the house, Danny is mostly quiet and curious. Occasionally he builds small fires, but you wouldn't call him a pyromaniac. He just likes to get close to the heat and watch the burning. One teacher had called him "sullen." Another said he was "angry at the world."

Danny knows anger, but he doesn't know what "sullen" means. His father scoffed at this teacher, saying over dinner one night, "She just doesn't understand you." His mother glared across the table. "Stop, Jim," she said, and his father just stared down at his plate.

After dinner, Danny plays his clarinet. He practices in his room, removed from his sisters' fights and tantrums. He cares deeply for the family dog, and cannot imagine that soon it will lie rotting on the kitchen floor, its carcass buzzing with flies.

Though he'll never admit it, he secretly, quietly idolizes his older sisters, even if he does mock their cackling and crying, their loud girlish ways. Just last week he sneaked a peek at Joleen's journal, all of it nonsense about boys and froufrou stuff and dreams of being a movie starlet.

She doesn't understand the threat that faces them all, not like Danny does. She just wants to be a pest, wants to ignore the fear. It drives him crazy sometimes, but Danny envies her innocent laugh and easygoing manner, her ability to ignore all the tension and see past what's right in front of her face. She's obliviously happy, like all children should be. Danny already knows that his sister will come out of this OK and feel little of the fallout that he internalizes deep in his marrow, the side effects of these days shaping and twisting his personality, pushing him toward the extreme edges of his consciousness.

After the apocalypse, Jim Dahlberg is angry, but he can't show it. He needs to be strong. He feels the skin around his neck tighten and swell, hot to the touch, and his knuckles ache. His words catch in his throat when he talks, quivering and sinking. He wants to scream and yell and curse his God, but the words won't rise.

This morning, Jim shoveled dirt from his pickup against the church foundation, fortifying it for shelter. He needs to focus on the work at hand, not the fear and panic in his fluttering chest. He suspects that his boy, Danny, can sense it. The boy understands him and has been even more silent and sullen these days, retreating to the cellar again, sitting alone in the dark and mumbling to himself. Jim wants to run, wants to grab his family and escape from what's coming, but he knows it is pointless. You can't outrun this kind of war. There is nowhere to go.

His back hurts, his shoulders too. He didn't sleep well the night before. People who know Jim know he's troubled. They can see it in his face. Normally he's the affable jokester, the jolly neighbor, but now his visage is carved into a granite mask. He looks like his teeth hurt.

"You OK?" a woman asked earlier that morning at the church, but Jim didn't even hear her. "Jim, you OK?" she had to ask again before he could respond.

"Just a little preoccupied," he said.

Jim was thinking about his wife, Eve, and the way she'd just left earlier after they argued about Denise's wedding. He was thinking how she just jumped in her car, said something about needing something from the mall, and drove off. She was gone for hours. And when she came back the Chevy was all dented up. She didn't buy anything, didn't have any shopping bags, and she didn't offer an explanation.

Jim was also thinking about the wedding they were supposed to plan. He was thinking about ceremony, pomp and circumstance, the little bride and groom atop the white cake. He was thinking about how it was all lost now. He was supposed to walk his daughter down the aisle, giving her away to the boy she loves, the medical student with a promising future. He was prepared to be the proud father of the bride. But today his tuxedo hangs in its plastic bag in his closet.

Eve is in denial still, and she won't stop planning the wedding in her head, going over details. He wants to tell her, "There won't be any damn wedding." But he's already said this and she won't listen. Everything is wrong. Nothing makes sense.

Jim Dahlberg is not a highly educated man. He was a soldier in Vietnam, a grunt drafted young who'd seen the horrors of conventional war. A man who'd committed horrors, done bad things to people, and tried to forget, tried to leave it all behind. He doesn't want to remember that pain.

Jim doesn't have a lot of letters after his name, but he knows things about people and the world. He listens and reads and pays attention. Jim understands that things between the U.S. and the Soviet Union don't get this far along without something bad happening. He sees it coming.

He'd been raised on the Cold War, drilled at school on preparations for attacks, his head tucked between his knees, believing firmly that they could survive. He knows about the missile silos ringing the city, just a few miles from the family farm, but he didn't think they would ever be used. He knows about the flat, unobtrusive sentinels with their atomic payloads, their twelve-foot fences topped with razor wire. He knows these things but doesn't like to talk about them. Jim wants to protect his family and feels foolishly guilty for not doing more, for not taking them away from all of the tension or at least explaining things better for Danny. The boy knows more than the girls. Danny understands the fear, the danger of living in a targeted place.

Jim Dahlberg—father, farmer, husband, former soldier—wants to do more than speak out at a town meeting, more than sit and listen to that damn preacher whining and carrying on. Jim wants to show the audience how he can play the guitar and sing, his voice warbling like a songbird. He wants people to see him holding his wife, the two of them embracing on the bulb-lit porch of their country home, because Jim Dahlberg is more than a simple farmer in a complicated story.

New Mutations

AFTER MY PARENTS dropped the divorce on us, I had to leave our house. I had to get away. I didn't get far, but I still managed to disappear. I just picked up my basketball, drifted outside, and as darkness fell and the floodlights came on, I ran all over the cracked driveway shooting jumpers and layups, free throws and fadeaways. I stayed out there, lost in the movement, until Dad opened the door and called to me.

"It's late," he said. "You should come in. We should talk about this."

I listened. But I didn't feel like talking. I knew my life had changed forever. I knew that one world had ended, another had begun, and I would have to adapt. In some ways, I grew up instantly that night.

I thought to myself, *You're on your own now.* I'd read enough books and seen enough movies to know that child independence usually begins with a parent's death, or at least recognition of his parents' fallibility.

In the days that followed, basketball became a comforting escape for me, a way to get out of the house, away from messy thoughts and emotions. There was an easy logic to the sport that soothed me. I could retreat to my own little world free of adults, without pressure to talk, emote, or anything—just the simple, repetitive physical task of putting a leather ball through a metal hoop.

The basketball court became my new post-apocalyptic landscape, a blank page with defined edges, boundaries, and rules, a place for imagining. Within its lines, I developed elaborate fantasies of escape and heroism that usually centered around me being "discovered" by Larry Brown, the coach of the Kansas Jayhawks, as I practiced in the driveway. Usually I was invited to join the team as a special kind of exception, an object lesson in the importance of hard work and dedication. I was the Rudy of college basketball, the kid with little talent but a giant, superhero-sized heart. Of course there were the obligatory last-second-shot scenarios, the game-winning free throws in overtimes, and the cover photo on *Sports Illustrated*. I spent hours and hours escaping in my driveway or to the caged-in courts of local playgrounds.

Within the boundaries of the court, I could find a kind of freedom and structure, a shape to my life that wasn't dependent on my parents, my teachers, or anyone else. I shoveled snow to clear a space sometimes. I learned discipline by practicing over and over and over again to hit a turnaround jump shot like Larry Bird, or a hook shoot like Patrick Ewing.

Sports Illustrated took the place of my comic books as a seminal text, providing for me the lingua franca of late adolescence. In those pages, I found new heroes—people like Bird, Dr. J, Magic, Ewing, and Barkley—and I learned how to communicate with my peers. I learned how to man-talk.

I also learned to adapt in my own way, learned to become like many of my superhero role models who lived in two different worlds, with two different identities. My parents, despite some serious animosity that existed between them, narrowly averted dragging Matt and me into divorce court, managing to agree that they should share custody. But this wasn't the sort of joint custody arrangement other kids had. We didn't just spend the weekend with Dad, we divided the week in half.

The new rhythm of our lives went like this: Monday through Wednesday until noon was Mom's time, and Wednesday afternoon through Friday night was Dad's time. Then we alternated homes every other weekend. I had two bedrooms, two dressers, two sets of clothes, and two faces—one for Dad's house and one for Mom's, sort of like the mutant Janus from *Thundarr the Barbarian* with his fancy double-shielded helmet, or Two-Face Harvey Dent in *Batman*, the good man scarred by loss and fire and left with one good and handsome white-knight half-face and one melted and badly disfigured half-face. Like the chameleon in our fourth-grade classroom, I learned to blend in and adapt. I learned to take on new forms, new identities, new colors, and new faces after the divorce.

One face was for the lawless post-apocalyptic terrain of my father's house, where we rode motorcycles in the front yard and the shrubs grew wild and untamed, and another face for my mom's house of order, rules, and stability. One was for the boys at school, and another for myself. I learned how to adapt and talk about sports and pretend like all I wanted in the world was to shoot a turnaround fadeaway like Bird or throw a pass like Elway—even if the truth was that I wanted to write novels like Tolkien and short stories like Ambrose Bierce, even if I wanted to spend hours drawing and using architectural stencils to design elaborate underground houses, or maybe just bore you to death with a minute-by-minute timeline of the events on the day Lincoln was assassinated.

In some ways the lingering fallout from my parents' divorce was harder to handle than the immediate impact of the news. I felt like I was dealing with it as well as could be expected. I was adjusting, adapting, and moving forward. But suddenly a lot of people acted very concerned about my emotions and ideas. This would be the first time in my life, but not the last, that people close to me admitted they were afraid of me.

They seemed to think that I was a ticking time bomb, a roiling kettle of emotions and angst, and I suppose they were right. But I'd been like that for as long as I could remember, and I couldn't understand why now they were so interested in what I had to say. Sure, I spent a lot of time at my desk in the hallway because I couldn't sit still in class or shut up or stop myself from saying things I shouldn't to the teacher. Sure, I wrote angry screeds in my journal about my teacher, comparing her to a Nazi, and created an elaborate fantasy novel in my head featuring a boy named Jaryd trapped in an underground dungeon. But that didn't mean I was troubled. That didn't mean I needed some kind of intervention, I thought.

The school counselor took me out for ice cream once and tried to get me to talk about my feelings, but I'm lactose-intolerant and I've never trusted people who are excessively nice to my face—especially when I know they're saying things behind my back like "scary," "weird," "big," and "sullen."

The more adults demanded that I talk and tell them what I was thinking, the more I wanted to remain silent. In the silence, my imagination began to fill in the gaps, invent stories, histories, and myths to make sense of it all. In the silence I saw Danny Dahlberg and the ripples emanating out from him. Some days I would crawl inside my closet, slide the door closed until only a single band of light penetrated the darkness, and drift outside myself, into nowhere and nothingness, sinking into the inky black calm and quiet, onto the cold linoleum floor, imagining that I was the only boy left on the planet.

There Is No Nowhere

LIKE THE TALE of my parents' divorce, much of the narrative in *The Day After*, the story behind the apocalypse, is only overheard in bits and pieces of dialogue, fragments of conversations and speeches. Most of the detail is broadcast as background noise over the televisions and radios the characters have turned on for news. There is no voice-over narrator providing guidance, authority, and direction. The light is dim and it's hard to read the meaning.

The movie opens with brief introductions to several different families. Two of these families—the Dahlbergs and the Gallatins—are about to be united by a marriage of their children, Bruce and Denise. We see Denise sneak out of the house at night, climb onto Bruce's motorcycle, and ride off. We see the two of them returning in the morning, Denise sneaking back into the house, her little sister Joleen spying all the way.

Elsewhere, Dr. Oaks and his wife, Helen, talk in the kitchen about their daughter, Marilyn, and how she can't or won't communicate with her mother. Helen winds her watch as they talk, and when she is finished he helps her clasp it on her wrist, agreeing to talk with their daughter, to find out what's going on.

Viewers get a superficial slice of various lives, a snapshot of numerous everyday experiences, just enough to see what's at stake, a quick spatter of characterization—mostly superficial foreshadowing and positioning of props—before the bombs drop and change everything.

There is no Danny Dahlberg guiding us through it all. We get oblique, confusing bits of conversations, transmissions that easily escape attention. In a perhaps misguided effort to understand this time in my own life, I watch the movie over and over again, jotting down bits of dialogue, images, fragments of speech—hoping that it will all coalesce into something meaningful.

There are so many incongruities.

In one early scene, we find Dr. Russell Oaks, played by Jason Robards, touring the Spencer Art Museum on KU's campus. For some reason, he's drinking from a carton of milk when he meets his daughter outside.

In my viewing notes it reads: "Milk? This doesn't make sense." But little of this makes sense.

The museum is a place I visited numerous times as a school kid, but a place that, in the reality of the movie, was supposed to be the Nelson Art Museum in Kansas City. Neither place sells milk by the carton, as far as I know, and even if they did, who would drink a carton of milk on a hot summer day?

Dr. Oaks walks around the museum with his daughter—a woman wearing ridiculously huge eyeglasses, a woman who, we will learn, was conceived on the eve of the Cuban Missile Crisis, in 1962, in a hotel room in New York—conceived, it would seem, on another brink of possible nuclear war.

Father and daughter stop briefly in front of a painting of a pasty-faced English gentleman in a white wig holding a finger to his lips. *Shhhhhhh*, he seems to say. *Don't mention the obvious.* They continue to stroll as she tells her father of her plans to move to Boston, and they stop in front of a landscape painting.

The daughter says, "The artist wants you to be in the landscape."

"You mean a God's-eye view?" Dr. Oaks responds, and because this bit of dialogue is left to float there, detached from character and context, we know we're supposed to hear the symbolism, the weight of metaphor.

THE HENDRYS, a simple farm family who happen to live next door to a missile silo, have gathered at the table for breakfast. The mother in her apron, the father in his overalls, no shirt, rippling muscles. The children sit at the table, waiting, as Mr. Hendry slides up behind Mrs. Hendry, grabs her around the waist, and whispers something in her ear.

"But what about the biscuits?" she protests, but she is already loosening her apron strings.

He drags her by the hand, out of the kitchen, upstairs to the bedroom. They leave the children to the biscuits.

THE BLACK SOLDIER tries to comfort his wife as he's packing to leave Sedalia. He's been called up, pressed into duty. He doesn't really know what's happening, but he knows it isn't good. His wife doesn't want him to go. The baby is crying and he's hardly home anymore. She just wants the family to stay together. Can't he just stay? Can't he just not go? But that isn't an option. He's a soldier. This is what he does. This is his job. He can't think about her and the baby.

WHEN I CONTACTED Nicholas Meyer, I tried to get him to tell me stories about shooting the film that summer of 1982. I was looking for some behind-the-melodrama drama. I was looking for catfights and confirmation of rumors about Robards being drunk and disorderly in downtown restaurants. I was looking for moments of petulance from Steve Guttenberg, perhaps some conflict with the hardworking and humble John Cullum, or just a moment when the Broadway-trained actor broke out into song on the set, just to loosen things up.

Instead, Meyer told me that the real challenge on the set was dealing with the toll their roles were taking on the actors' psyches. He mentioned that Guttenberg suffered what they called "nuke-mares" and had trouble sleeping during the filming.

"Actors," he said, "have the fourth-toughest job in the country, after police, firefighters, and EMTs."

"Really?"

"Oh yeah," he said, and I got the feeling that this was something he liked to say a lot.

Because we, the citizens of Lawrence, didn't choose our role, I asked Meyer if Guttenberg or the other actors had chosen their roles because of the anti-nuke message. He told me that he knew Amy Madigan and Jason Robards had definitely chosen the film for political reasons. He offered the role to Robards on an airplane, and he quoted Robards as saying, "Hey, it beats signing petitions." He also said he didn't think that Guttenberg was very political. I reminded him that Guttenberg had at one time been the honorary mayor of Pacific Palisades, California, that he had actually been Meyer's mayor.

Meyer hesitated for a moment, then said, "I think the title 'honorary' tells you all you need to know about the political significance of that role."

It *is* interesting to consider the emotional trauma those actors must have faced working on *The Day After*. They lived in that imagined reality for a long time. I see why they might have been haunted. For many of us, the nuke-mare didn't end when the cameras stopped rolling, just as for Meyer and my parents and others it didn't end when they ducked under their desks.

IN ANOTHER SNAPSHOT, Joe Huxley, played by John Lithgow, sits in a downtown Lawrence barbershop, reading a magazine. It's a very quaint sort of scene—the small-town barbershop and casual conversation among men—set in the exact same place where I'd gotten my hair cut and listened to the back-and-forth banter between barbers and customers. But the conversation is not so lighthearted today, not so easy in these days. They're not bullshitting about sports or other trivia. They're talking about the increasing tensions between the U.S. and the Soviet Union. They're talking about war.

Our young fiancé, Bruce, announces he is getting his last haircut as a "free man." He tells the other men he's getting married tomorrow. He says this with the happy-go-lucky guilelessness of a boy announcing that he's getting his driver's license. Ollie, the barber, congratulates him. It all seems so innocent.

Joe Huxley is different. He clearly isn't there for a haircut. He sits behind Bruce and the barbers, his long legs stretched out. His shaggy hair hangs down over his ears. The barbers wear blue shirts. They silently *snip-snip*, pretending to cut hair, tolerating Huxley's banter.

Playing the part well, John Lithgow holds a copy of *Sports Illustrated* and comments on the rising political tensions and nuclear threat facing America. He delivers Huxley's lines sarcastically, with a kind of detached awareness, a psychological distance that suggests some knowledge or authority in the matter.

A presidential news conference plays on the radio in the background.

Huxley says, "They'll tell us what they want us to hear."

He talks about how it's really no longer a question of *when* but *where*. Troops are amassing in Germany. Conflict is inevitable. It's only a matter of time. Conversation continues in the shop and Bruce looks stricken, as if he has been overcome with nausea or shot in the gut. He stares into the mirror, his face washed with confusion. He doesn't really understand. He looks utterly dumbfounded.

"What do you think the chances are of something like that happening way out here in the middle of nowhere?" Bruce asks, expressing the same sort of question I was asking my parents.

"Nowhere!" Huxley scoffs. "There is no nowhere anymore. You're sitting right next to the Whiteman Air Force Base and about 150 Minuteman missiles spread from here to Sedalia."

He pauses for dramatic effect.

The camera focuses tight on Lithgow's bespectacled face. In his characteristic lilting speech, he says, "That's a whole lotta bull's-eyes," and the last part of the word, the "-eyes," stretches out and flattens, then hangs in the air for a second. Lithgow is really good at delivering a line. He makes it stick in your head like a tune. No matter what you do, you can't shake it. The refrain hangs around in the ether of your subconscious for a while.

WHEN THE MISSILES erupt from the horizon all around Lawrence, rising from invisible nests, trailing feathers of white smoke, all of it is accomplished with appropriately spooky special effects.

After this, scenes of familiar characters are spliced together with stock footage of nuclear tests, giving the entire thing a sort of collage or documentary feel. It's Nicholas Meyer, the final editor of these scenes, who is doing all the work. Actors become props, fuel, cinders. People are vaporized, buildings are reduced to sticks, and cars are disabled by the electromagnetic pulse, left stranded on the highway. As people emerge from their vehicles and begin to walk, the soundtrack emits a constant, low ticking rumble as orange-black mushroom clouds bloom over Kansas City.

The bombs arrive in a rapid succession of concussive images, a kind of shotgun blast to the senses. A low static hum emits from the television, punctuated with booming thunder, the roar of fire, and an intermittent twitter of human screams layered in over a roar of wind or a freight train. More mushrooms bloom, popping up all over the landscape, rising and lingering in the sky like sculpture.

IT'S NOT UNTIL years later that I would be able to watch this sequence of the film all the way through, and I still have trouble viewing it without flinching just a bit. The film is washed in red. It bounces quickly from image to image: *Woman standing on the street, mouth agape. Man walking. Couple at the marriage altar. Woman holding her baby. Crowds of people shopping or dining. A classroom full of children. The white horse. The entire Hendry family. Old couple walking hand in hand down a country lane.*

One by one the innocent people are *skeletonized*—which is the only word I can think of to describe this special effect. It's as if their images have been taken by an X-ray camera and all you see is their animated upright bones, struck down in mid-motion. Seeing this as a kid, I wondered if that's what a blast would do—just strip all the skin and meat from your body, leave your skeleton standing there at a crosswalk.

Would we just find piles of bleach-white bones, teeth, and dust—maybe the occasional skull? I'd heard bizarre and troubling stories about shadows of people being burned into the pavement of Hiroshima, and I imagined my neighbors and friends pressed into the concrete, the outlines of my classmates scarred into the playground. That fact alone has always made the average random shadow seem more significant to me—like the possible last impression I could leave.

The filmmakers took images, scenes, and characters that had already been established and simply repeated them—like the white horse galloping through the green pasture—then they *skeletonized* them for effect. They *skeletonized* the soldier's wife holding their baby, Dr. Oaks's daughter too. Helen Oaks standing in her kitchen. They did the same to the public street scenes, suggesting "It could be you," and—in a particularly heinous scene that still bothers me today—they included that image of a classroom full of children, the kids sitting obediently at their desks. Kendall Meade is there, smiling in the back, holding his special heart. They are not under their desks, not hidden away in a basement shelter, and all of them are vaporized, reduced to bones, disintegrated.

After this we see stock film footage of atomic bomb tests, churning black waves of flame and smoke and fallout; trees whipping back and forth, stripped and pulverized; debris hurtling through the air in massive roiling clouds; houses flattened like paper houses—houses that are clearly prop houses.

With the only working hospital in the region, Lawrence immediately becomes a place of refuge for blast victims, a place of hope and possible salvation—just like it's always been. The highways—clogged with disabled cars—become trails into town, but we are quickly over-whelmed by the tide of survivors and we struggle mightily with vio-lence and lawlessness, with simple human decency. Before long, refu-gee tent cities have sprouted up in the grassy knolls of South Park and the rest of downtown, by the old train and beneath the bridge over the Kaw, along with piles of brick rubble, smoke wafting through the air; a blackened body buried, charred to a crisp, face frozen in terror; and the silence of cornflake fallout drifting in the breeze.

Starlet Night

AS A RECOVERING teen, still stung by the apocalypse, I believed Ellen Anthony to be the most spectacular and exotic girl in all of West Junior High School. Some of this had to do with her big role in *The Day After* as Joleen Dahlberg, the precocious younger daughter of Jim Dahlberg.

Some of my belief had to do with the fact that she probably *was* the most spectacular and exotic girl in all of West Junior High School. No offense to anyone, but Ellen was beautiful and smart and talented. She'd been in a major motion picture. She'd survived the fake apocalypse, and I figured it was just a matter of time before she was starring in cereal commercials, sitcoms, daytime dramas, or big budget action comedies. Given the hype surrounding the movie, I figured she'd soon be meeting with presidents and diplomats. She was like local royalty.

Ellen had numerous on-screen appearances in *The Day After* and several important speaking parts before she sort of disappeared from the story. One of her big scenes involved her stealing her older sister's vaginal diaphragm contraceptive and hiding it as her sister, Denise, chases her around the house.

She also had one of the more famous, or at least personally resonant, lines in the movie when she tugs on her father's sleeve and asks, "There's not going to be a war, is there, Daddy?"

A lot of kids wondered the same thing—and Ellen asked the question for all of us.

When I finally met Ellen, after the movie had aired and the hype mostly blown over, she was sweet and humble and unassuming in all the ways you hope a movie star will be but rarely is. More importantly, she liked me. I could never figure out why, but after some awkward flirting and strained phone calls, she invited me to sneak out of my dad's house and meet her late one night. Our love . . . or, uh, romance (if it can be called that) . . . would not be one that flourished in the light of day.

"Just come late and knock on my window," she told me, and I nearly melted.

Was this really happening?

Some of the rush of the experience was tempered by the fact that in the post-divorce landscape of my dad's house, I was allowed to "sneak out" as long as I told him about it first. This, of course, took some of the shine off the illicit feelings and rebelliousness. But I didn't care. I was out of the house, headed for a possibly romantic rendezvous with a movie starlet. I didn't need rules to make this feel dangerous.

I liked wandering through the empty streets of Lawrence. I felt like I was on the verge of being the only person alive on the planet, that if the stars didn't look quite right or the sun was slow to rise, I'd be the only one to notice. It's probably an exaggeration to say I felt like a sole survivor, but it's a fine line between sleep and death sometimes, and the streetlights drooping their dreamy glow over the blacktop seemed almost otherworldly, like Orson Welles's spaceships descending on the town to vaporize us all with their laser beams. It wasn't so much fear I felt as the adrenaline rush of danger.

I made it to Ellen's house, knocked gently on her basement window, and waited for her to appear. When she did, I held Ellen in my arms, and we leaned up against her stepfather's car and kissed in the innocent, awkward way that teenagers kiss, until our lips hurt and we just had to quit.

Though I didn't have much experience at that point, I was convinced that Ellen was the best kisser in the entire world. I'm sure I was positively nightmarish in that department, and I take this opportunity to apologize. My only other practice had come with a big-mouthed girl who wore braces and had a tongue that was fat and pink and lolled around her mouth like some sort of farm animal's tongue. What I lacked in technique I hopefully made up for in enthusiasm. If I was completely repulsive, Ellen was graceful enough not to let me know.

I left after a few minutes of kissing, just kissing, and watched her disappear into her house and return to bed. I started my walk home through the barren streets of Lawrence and nearly danced across the asphalt and concrete, still buzzing from adrenaline and hormones and tingling lips. It was easily the most romantic and exciting experience

I'd had yet with a girl. I felt more alive than I thought was possible and wanted to sing or scream or something.

As I stepped up to cross Iowa Street, the last main thoroughfare before home, a police car floated through the intersection, hanging in the space between me and the other side, between safety and me. I saw the officer's massive head turn and spot me, and I could almost hear his automatic brain clanking. *Curfew violation.* I froze for a second on the corner as his brake lights flared bright red—and then I took off running as fast as I could across the street.

I hit the opposite curb and turned to see the cop flip a U-turn in the middle of the street, his headlights swinging around like two incandescent cannons, their beams searching wildly for me. I tucked my head and ran, cutting diagonally across one street and turning down another. I felt his lights stalking me. I ran and ran and, just as the car turned the corner to follow me, I dropped to my knees and crawled between two parked cars, wedging my body under the front bumper of one.

The cop slowed, turned on to the side street, and stopped. He flipped on his ultra-bright spotlight and worked it back and forth, up and down the street like a machine. Gravel bit into my back and my heart thumped against my ribcage. My face pressed against a plastic bumper, my legs tucked into a ball, I tried to act like the roly-poly bugs in our yard with their impenetrable shells, their little heads tucked away.

The cop just sat there. His light played over the street and I could feel it panning over the cars where I was hiding, the projected heat of it burning my back. I was sure he'd seen me, but after a moment or two of silent watching, he switched the light off, turned around, and drove away.

I lay there between the cars for a few minutes afterward, giving him a chance to get far away, and for me to catch my breath. Adrenalin coursed through my veins and I felt like I was plugged into an electrical outlet. I began to imagine all the horrible things that would have happened to me in the hands of the cop. I saw him sucking me into his car, restraining me, asking me all sorts of probing questions. Then I saw the two of us standing on the porch of my father's house, the cop holding the scruff of my shirt in his meaty paw and asking, "Is this your son, sir?" And I saw the look of disappointment on my father's face when I admitted that I didn't tell him I was sneaking out, that I had broken his rule.

As I ran the last two blocks home, I wasn't sure how I felt. Frightened. Elated. I was still a scared, awkward kid. I was still the two-faced child of divorce. I was still all the things I'd been before, but there was also something exceptional about kissing a starlet in the moonlight and running from the cops—however briefly—that made me feel like a superhero, or perhaps an antihero, a super-villain, at least someone special. I seemed to slide out of my body, separate, and see it all from above—as if I had been a camera filming the chase, following the boy as he flees from the police and hides, heart pounding, and barely makes it home to his basement bedroom.

12

DAHLBERG VARIATION

Danny Dahlberg is tired of canned food. He misses his clarinet. And the stink coming from upstairs is almost unbearable. He knows he'll have to step over the dog to get out and probably have to help his dad get the carcass out of the kitchen. But besides that, he's adapting to their life underground. It feels OK to him. He's been fantasizing about living in an underground house for a couple of years now—ever since all of this fear-mongering about the apocalypse began, or perhaps ever since his father told him of the hole he'd dug in his yard in Western Kansas during the height of the Red scares of the '50s.

Danny often visited the office supply store for graph paper and mechanical pencils, spending hours staring at all the different writing utensils, the wide assortment of erasers, and the architectural stencils with cutouts for toilets, bathtubs, trees, sliding glass, and swinging doors.

His drawings are all upstairs now, crammed into the drawers of his desk. He'd designed at least three complete homes, customized with skylights, elevators and emergency staircases, solar panels, water tanks, and backup generators—all of it painstakingly drawn in minute detail. The later sketches featured crude drawings of native grasses and shrubbery, a few earthen berms and water features—all from a time when Danny had more faith in the surface. But now he wonders if he'll just be living in the basement forever.

He's heard mice scurrying around in the walls again, their little claws making a ruckus in the dark, and he wonders if they'll survive, or if they'll mutate from the radiation and fallout. Perhaps they'll become super-mice, mutant rodents who know karate. He thinks they'll probably just die in the walls, and when they do they'll begin to stink like the dog upstairs.

Danny has started having nightmares again about fires, and he woke up this morning drenched in sweat. His teeth ache and his eyes feel crusty and weird. He's begun to see a fuzzy white spot at the edge of his right eye, and he thinks it's getting bigger. He thinks maybe his eyes are beginning to heal themselves. His father has been listening to the radio and says they can leave when the rad count drops.

"How long, Daddy?" Joleen pushes.

"He don't know. Didn't you hear him?" Danny says.

"Shut, up Danny. Just shut up," she yells at him. "I hate you!"

The basement is quiet for a moment as her words linger.

"Joleen!" Daddy barks. "Watch your mouth. Danny's right. I don't know. We just have to wait and see."

Joleen is dumb. She doesn't know any better. She thinks it's all a game. Danny can't blame her. It's not like anyone has really explained things to them—at least not in a way that makes sense. They are all tired of waiting. They can't hide down there forever. Danny knows this. Joleen knows this too.

A day or so later, after they've emerged from the cellar, Danny stands at the kitchen sink in their home with his two sisters and his mother, waiting for his father to return from a meeting with the agricultural agent. They are washing and cutting potatoes, prepping for a family dinner, acting for the first time in days as if everything were normal, when Jim Dahlberg rolls up to the far gate in his horse-drawn buggy.

The light above the sink shines on Danny's face. He can feel its warmth but still sees no light in his eyes, nothing that pierces the blackness he has come to know. He rolls a potato in his hands, washing it in the water, and listens to his sisters and mother talk. They cannot see out the window; the glare from the light obscures their view. They cannot see the squatter family out by the gate, the dirty-faced kids sitting on the dead cow. But Danny can see them.

He can imagine them, picture them in his head. He can see it all in his mind's eye as it happens.

Danny heard the squatters earlier when he stepped outside for a moment; he smelled the smoke from their fire, heard their voices drifting up on a breeze, and he was afraid. His mother hustled him inside and told him not to pay any attention to them, but he knew they were there. Waiting.

He turns off the water and cocks his ear to the window. He thinks he recognizes the sound of his father's voice and wonders if he will invite the squatters inside, wonders if he'll even stop or just keep moving home, back to Danny and his sisters and his mother. It's is the kind of thing his dad would do. He would try to help the squatters if things weren't already so bad.

Please keep moving, Daddy, he pleads silently.

Out by the gate, Jim Dahlberg has reached his breaking point. He can't hide it any longer, can't take it anymore. He just wants to get home to his family, to a dinner with his kids and some pleasant conversation after another long day in the post-apocalyptic world. But these squatters are sitting on his goddamn dead cow, his milk cow, for god's sake, and they don't seem to even notice that they're on his property, his land. Jim slumps over in his seat, his joints aching and creaking.

"Now listen," he says. "You all are going to have to move along."

The squatter family stares at him—dirty-faced, silent, and sullen. They appear almost animal.

Jim climbs down from the wagon and approaches them. As he does, one of the men stands and slips around to his periphery, lurking just outside the frame.

"Did y'all hear me?" Jim asks.

Nobody says a word. One man stares up at him. The children too. Jim cannot see the other man sneaking up behind him. He doesn't see it coming, but Danny hears it. The pause. The possibilities. The scuff of a boot on the gravel. The squatter raises his shotgun and shoots Jim in the side and back. Jim twists and drops with a quick dull thump to the earth. The squatter children don't move from their seat on the cow. They just stare. They do not cry or flinch or act as if anything unusual has happened.

In the house, beneath the light, Danny shudders at the gunshot. His mother and sisters gasp and cup their hands to their mouths.

"Jim!" his mother screams and runs out the door.

The ripples from that noise—of his father's body hitting the dirt— spread through his mind, the waves crashing up against other pictures now fading, slowly washed away by the truth. It's all over now. Their family is gone. Jim is dead.

13

This Is Lawrence

IN THE DARK days afterward, we find Joe Huxley again. He's sequestered in a shadowy science lab of a campus building at the University
of Kansas. There seem to be students gathered there too, hiding from
the fallout in the dark. Huxley, played by John Lithgow, is no longer
smug and sarcastic, no longer so far removed from the apocalyptic
reality. A dim light glints off his glasses. He looks defeated, sunken,
and sad.

Speaking into a short-wave CB radio, he pauses between each
utterance to release the button and says:

Hello?

(click)

Hello?

(click)

Is anybody there?

(click)

Is anybody there?

(click)

*This is Lawrence. This is Lawrence, Kansas. Is anybody there? Anyone
at all?*

(click)

*This is Joe Huxley. I'm broadcasting from the science building at the
University of Kansas. Is anybody there?*

(click)

I have an atmosphere report for anybody who's listening.

(click)

Dr. Oaks, played by Jason Robards, is listening. He may be the only
one left listening, and he's just a mile away, taking a moment to himself
in the Douglas County Hospital. Dr. Oaks answers him, and Huxley
reports the radiation levels are higher than he expected, speculating
that Lawrence is getting fallout from "Titan missile bases in Wichita."

Dr. Oaks asks Huxley when it might be safe to move people from one building to another.

Huxley, with much acid in his voice, says, "It'll *never* be safe."

The camera focuses again on his bespectacled face. One of the lenses in his glasses is cracked. You don't really wonder how a nuclear blast manages to crack a scientist's glasses, because the movie is populated with unexplainable head wounds, burns, and injuries. (Not only did the people in this film suffer a nuclear attack, but they were also the victims of an unprecedented scourge of car accidents, random burnings, and beatings.)

The camera stays close up on his face. Joe Huxley's lips and chin stand out in relief; the round bright dome of his nose pokes out into the darkness. Dr. Oaks encourages him not to give up hope.

Huxley asks, *Have you, uh, picked up anyone else out there on your end?*

(click)

Not a soul, comes the reply.

(click)

This is Lawrence, Huxley says. *Is anybody there?*

(click)

This is Lawrence, Kansas.

(click)

Is anybody there?

(click)

Anybody at aaalllll?

(click)

Lithgow stretches out the last part of "all" so much that it sounds anguished, desperate, and utterly alone. His voice. These lines. They too echo through the movie for me, filling up any spaces or silence. Lawrence is the last place on earth, it seems, the only place sending signals out into the void.

THE ROLLING TEXT at the end of *The Day After* reads, in part, "Nuclear war is horrible and survival in its wake is abhorrent, even unimaginable, to civilized humanity." It's telling, I suppose, that *The Day After* was criticized by many, Carl Sagan among them, for being entirely too optimistic and not nearly as realistic as it should have been given its ambition to shock the public into action—like the paddles of a defibrillator jolting our collective heart. Critics argued that the movie did not, in fact, go far enough to portray the absolute devastation and annihilation that a nuclear attack would cause. They said the movie didn't frighten us enough.

In the days after, Lawrence rapidly deteriorates into a place of lawlessness and violence. Before long, the simple trappings of civilization collapse and we are faced with the reality of refugee tent cities in our parks, mass graves piled with bodies, and firing squads lined up to punish looters.

In the face of nuclear war, people lose their cars, their electricity, their drinking water. Worst of all, they lose their humanity—even the exceptionally humane and good country people of Kansas. They lose their innocence and their empathy—those things that make them who they are—or at least some of them do.

Because the Dahlbergs sheltered him in their basement, Stephen Klein, the college boy played by Guttenberg, has pledged to look after the Dahlberg children. After he leaves Danny in the hospital, he makes his way to the basketball gym, the historic Allen Fieldhouse, which has been converted into a triage center, convalescent home, and morgue. Beneath the red-and-blue bleachers and the banners for Big Eight championships, spread out over the hardwood, are hundreds and hundreds of cots.

He has come to find Denise, to just be with her and let her know that Danny had made it to the hospital. He stumbles into the gym, his hair reduced to a few long strands stitched to his bald head, his face dirty. He carries a rifle. He stumbles around amid the maze of cots, people dying everywhere he turns, and finally finds Denise. Her face is blotched with red sores and her teeth have begun to fall out. Her hair, what's left of it, wraps her liver-spotted skull like a vaporous cloud. But she smiles when she sees Stephen, smiles when he bends down close to her, holds her in his arms, and tells her that Danny is safe, that everything will be all right.

14

Final Gift

Toward the end of their lives, both of my grandparents called the Kiowa County Memorial Hospital in Greensburg home. In their final years, they were forced to abandon the house where they'd lived for almost seventy years, but they didn't move far. In fact, they moved just a few blocks away. You could almost see their old house from their new home.

Shortly after their deaths, my dad and his sisters decided to sell the family cabin in Colorado—a place gifted to them by my grandfather's will, a place built by him and my father, mother, aunts, and uncles in 1963, a place where we retreated every summer, away from the Kansas heat, humidity, and flatness, a place that nurtured generations of family. They sold it at the peak of the market and made a nice chunk of change. But we also lost something—something priceless that was perhaps inevitably doomed—a sense of shared history, story, and connection.

When the tornado took Greensburg, it took some of that connection too. It wiped away the architecture of family, the structure and keystones of stories, and though a new place could be rebuilt, new memories made, they would never replace the old.

When my dad and I visited Greensburg that summer after the storm, we stopped at the hospital where both of his parents had lived out their last days. We waded through puddles of water, over piles of debris. Beds crowded the hallway and black mold crept up the drywall. After the tornado, the rains had come and stayed for days. Here and there lay the waterlogged bodies of stuffed animals—the left-behind toy pets of people who were, by that time, calling somewhere else home.

I ducked into a room not far from the one where my grandfather had died, and I saw written on a small dry-erase board these words of orientation for a patient with dementia, or Alzheimer's, like my grandmother:

Today is May 4, 2007.

They'd left the day standing. Permanent, perhaps. Or at least until the bulldozers came and pushed it all down. But forever etched into the memory of people who had been there and who'd witnessed the end—even if their brains couldn't quite make sense of it all.

NEAR THE END of *The Day After*, Oaks, our heroic doctor, is clearly dying from radiation sickness. His nurse, Nancy Bauer, died earlier, offscreen. Some sort of hemorrhage or aneurysm. Others are falling too. Dying and filling up the grave outside. The hospital halls are lined with desperate, sickened people, and the pregnant woman has already given birth. Even that does little to lift Dr. Oaks's spirits. There is nothing left for him to do. The blind boy with has bandages is screaming again. Always sitting up in bed and screaming. Nothing comforts him any longer. Dr. Oaks' white hair hangs from his scalp in errant wisps.

He decides that he wants to return home one last time. He makes his way to Kansas City in the back of a military transport truck. He stops first at the World War II memorial tower in Kansas City, only to find bodies strewn about, and then stumbles his way to the brick-strewn street that was his old neighborhood, his home. Everything is charred black. He sinks to his knees at the sight of it. In the dust and rubble he discovers his wife's wristwatch. The hands frozen. Time stopped.

He looks up and sees in the remnants of his home a family of squatters seated beneath a makeshift shelter. Dr. Oaks is angry at first. He yells at them, tells them to get out, to go away, but they have nowhere else to go. The children stare up at him.

The gaunt-faced father gazes up at him, raises his hand meekly, but he does not point a rifle at Dr. Oaks, does not threaten him. Instead he reaches out and offers a bright round orange. It's a final offering of life, a gift of fruit in the end.

BOOK 3 FALLOUT

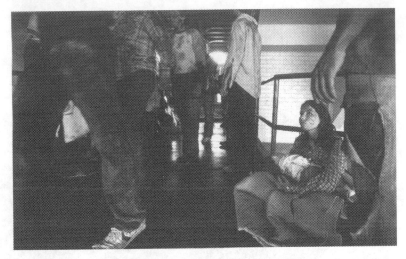

Mother and Child, Allen Fieldhouse, 1982

Triage in Allen Fieldhouse, 1982

We want to inspire public dialogue. What's most important is what happens after The Day After.

—Josh Baran, national media coordinator for Lawrence's nuclear disarmament movement, 1983

DAHLBERG VARIATION: *Red Dawn* Rising

The year is 1984, one year after. The story opens again on an average morning in an idyllic small town somewhere in the American West, far away from Lawrence—but not too far. Golden quaking aspen trees sway in the cool September breeze. It's the kind of mountain morning where cottony clouds spatter the bright blue canvas of the sky, birds chirp and twitter insistently, and children make their way inexorably to school—as if it were all part of a painting.

From the early pictures of citizens in town, driving trucks, smiling, and waving, we realize this is your standard Smalltown, America. But the camera is not focused long on the landscape.

The focus is on people, on characters—specifically, a group of good-looking high school boys in blue-and-yellow letter jackets, feathered hair, tight jeans, and muscle cars. Friends. Teammates. A circle of boys, just boys. Like me, Danny thinks.

He could be here too, part of this scene, but he'd be standing outside their circle most of the time, friends with a few individuals, always lingering in the margins. He plays sports too. He can speak their language, but he isn't really one of them. He's always been a curious boy, anxious and unsettled—more fearful than them. But he is not the main character in this story. He's a vehicle, a device of sorts. He is a lens.

Danny sees the pretty girls too as they move through the halls and classrooms, glowing, talking, some settling quietly and anonymously into seats nearby. But he doesn't talk with them like the other boys. He doesn't have that sort of confidence yet. He sits closer to the back of the room, next to the windows, because his eyes still aren't quite right and he needs the natural light. Today his eyes ache and throb. He takes his glasses off and sets them on his desk. He rubs his temples, squeezes the bridge of his nose. He closes his eyes and listens to the low hum of chatter, the rumble of voices blurring together into white noise. Mr. Teasdale, the only black person in the entire town, is talking again about the Mongol warriors and their siege strategy. He's a big man, but he's sweet and gentle. He cares for his kids. Danny has always appreciated the hypnotic timbre of his baritone voice. Danny often closes his eyes and just listens to Mr. Teasdale until he drifts off to sleep.

In this way, most days begin around here—and some mornings Danny remembers the past and wishes for something more.

Mr. Teasdale pauses as he speaks, stares out the window. Danny opens his eyes, looks up, gazes out the window too. Up in the sky, something is falling, blooming like a flower, a giant butterfly dropping. Dozens now. Not butterflies. Something bigger. Maybe large exotic birds, confused in their migration toward home. They come closer, softly falling.

Mr. Teasdale says it is very interesting and that they must have blown off course, way off course. It is not something beautiful and idyllic, not magical, as the figures fall into view and we see that they are not birds but paratroopers wearing snow-white camouflage, blue berets, and carrying automatic weapons. They scramble across the field, approaching the school, and someone says, "You better do something, Mr. Teasdale."

It still doesn't seem real. Danny thinks for a moment that this is just an exercise, a military training thing or some kind of special show for the ROTC kids. More parachutes drift down into the schoolyard. By now all of the students are crowded up to the window. Mr. Teasdale marches out of the room, down the hall, and out onto the playground. He's asking them, "What's going on here?" But the soldier screams *"No entiendo"* as he raises a machine gun and—just like it's nothing at all—sprays Mr. Teasdale with bullets. Big red spots bloom from his chest and everything goes crazy.

The paratrooper stands up, raises his rifle, aims it at the bank of windows, and opens fire, spraying bullets into the classroom. One kid, a boy Danny barely knows, gets shot in the face right away and falls on the window ledge next to him, blood oozing out of his skull, dripping down his face framed by shattered glass. This is an image Danny won't be able to forget.

Then it gets really noisy and messy. One of the soldiers fires an RPG down the hallway. Everyone screams and the windows explode with angry bees. Bullets *pock-pock-pock*ing into the walls all around. Kids dive under desks. Some run for cover. And Danny knows he should follow the football players out of the school, jump in the blue truck, and escape into the hills like Darrell and Matt and Arturo. He could join their band of freedom fighters. He could be a Wolverine too. He knows they have what it takes to survive, but Danny is still huddled under a desk when those other boys tear off in their Jeeps and trucks. He's still there, waiting, as he hears the shuffle of boots in the hallways, the barking of orders in Spanish, intermittent gunfire, and the crackle of military radio static.

He's still there, paralyzed by his own curiosity and his fascination with storms of violence, when the communist Cubans overtake the small-town high school and World War III begins. Danny sees it all. Danny is always there—letting us watch the end through different eyes. We only have to look hard enough to find him hiding in the margins.

The Man Behind the Curtain

IN THE SUMMER of 2006 a record-breaking heat wave struck California, killing almost two dozen people in the Central Valley alone, many of them in Fresno, where my wife, my son, and I had just relocated to from the East Coast (and Colorado before that). All the heat and death was enough to make me question our choice of a new home.

One old man in our neighborhood expired in his armchair when he refused to turn on his swamp cooler. He said the machine spoke to him, saying bad things; I thought I understood, since on some particularly hot days I could swear our oscillating fan was broadcasting Mexican *narcocorridos*. Air-conditioned city buses circulated around Fresno, picking up heat-stressed residents. We faced daily warnings of possible blackouts due to excessive power consumption.

Temperatures in Los Angeles soared well over the 100-degree mark for days on end, causing blackouts and a lot of collective angst. The nearby San Andreas Fault quivered continuously with potential. Fires raged in the suburban hills. The world seemed to be boiling, perhaps only moments away from full-on immolation.

Some days it felt like I was courting apocalypse, inviting it into my life again. I had, after all, just moved my family to a state that could, at least in the public imagination, slide off into the ocean with a few well-placed seismic events—and all of this was before the Greensburg tornado began to reveal a pattern in my life. At the time, I figured I needed to try and get closer to the end if I was ever to understand the whole story, so I decided to interview Nicholas Meyer.

WHEN I FOUND him, it was at his home in steaming hot Los Angeles, a house shaded in emerald green, hidden behind large, leafy eucalyptus trees, pines, and oleander—a property that looked as if it needed a gardener. Or napalm. But I appreciated the messiness. I would've been worried if it was too sterile, too clean and neat. Such order would be redundant in this part of Los Angeles.

The house sat along a busy four-lane road with a lush landscaped median, surrounded on all sides by enormous, sprawling blond "hognose" McMansions, their garages stretching out to the curb like hungry snouts.

Meyer's house instead featured an imposing red brick wall draped in thick vines and ivy that defined the perimeter, and a cheap red-and-black Beware of Dog sign hung on the gate. I couldn't tell if it was a lie, a facade designed to frighten intruders and unwanted guests, or if I should be genuinely afraid of a dog. In my neighborhood in Fresno, if you take such signs lightly it could mean your life or at least the loss of a limb.

I stood there on the sidewalk and couldn't discern a roofline of the house. There was no hint of one through the dense foliage. Just trees. No clues as the style of the house, the sort of personality the home might have. (Spanish? Italian? Modern? Postmodern?) It was somewhat inscrutable, but also oddly refreshing and welcoming among the showboats nearby—and it would take me a while to understand that the house was much like the man who owned it.

Traffic buzzed past, life coursing through the arteries of the big candy-coated city, a place that felt very far away from Kansas, even worlds away from Fresno. My teeth ached—something in the air, I guessed. I took a step back, out into the street, trying to collect myself and steel my nerves. Neighbors were probably wondering why the big sweaty guy in a loud plaid shirt was loitering in front of Nicholas Meyer's house.

I was there because I wanted to know why Meyer had made *The Day After* in the first place. It was, after all, a follow-up to his box office hit, *Star Trek: The Wrath of Khan*, and it was a TV movie, a lightning rod, and a potential career killer, and arguably his biggest public success until his recent screenplay adaptation of the Phillip Roth novel *Elegy*, a movie starring Ben Kingsley and Penelope Cruz.

The truth was that I wanted to see behind the curtain, behind his public comments about the movie and its meaning. I wanted to talk to the man who had re-created Kansas for me and for many others, a man whose story had overwritten Quantrill and Oz; I wanted to meet the new wizard.

The painted house number on the curb had faded and was peeling, barely legible, but I could read the addresses on either side and confirm that I had the right house. The *first* front gate was iron and easily opened, but then I was quickly faced with second wood-and-iron gate, thick as railroad ties and twelve feet tall. It looked like it was harvested from the ruins of a medieval castle. There was a keypad in the brick wall. I pressed the call button and a soft medium-pitched voice responded. "Yes?"

"Hi, um," I leaned closer to the metal box. "I, uh, I'm Steven Church here to meet with Nick Meyer."

"OK," the voice said, lower this time. "What I'm going to need you to do is go around to the side gate. You can park there. Or you can park in the driveway."

I left my car on the side street, walked around of the corner lot, and saw a second monolithic gate with another keypad. I waited for a moment or two, not sure if I should press the call button again. I pressed it. But then the gate started to open slowly, mechanically. As it swung out, I saw a short, tanned barefoot man standing next to a control panel, his hand on a button.

I always pictured Meyer as a tall, imposing figure, the kind of man you notice because he seems wound up tight like a rubber band and ready to snap; but he was densely packed, physically fit with hawkish features, salt-and-pepper hair, and piercing blue-gray eyes. He seemed relaxed too, deeply tanned and handsome; he looked Mediterranean, like a Greek sailing captain, and his bare feet made it seem like he'd just stepped off an ocean vessel of some kind.

I walked through the gate and it swung close behind me. Meyer strolled over and extended his hand. He wore a white T-shirt and kha-kis, and he walked slightly duck-footed.

"Hi," he said, nodding his head slightly. At first I couldn't be sure it was Meyer. He didn't look like the old pictures I'd seen. He was smaller than I expected. And, quite frankly, nicer than I expected.

When I smiled, shook his hand, and thanked him for having me, he said, "Oh, sure. Sure. I mean, I want you to get your money's worth. You came a long way. I want you to get whatever it is you need. We'll sit down. We'll talk. You can ask me some questions."

This was refreshing, as I'd heard a story about his crew shoot-ing a scene near the end of the film, one staged at Allen Fieldhouse

and featuring hundreds of local extras. On-screen we see Steve Guttenberg's character, Stephen Klein, stumbling in, searching for the
dying Denise Dahlberg amid the masses of sick citizens. It's a scene in
which, during the filming, an uncontrollable giggle spread through
the crowd and—as the story has been told to me—Meyer, clearly
frustrated, barked, "Now what I want is no movement, no talking . . .
nothing!"

The extras listened.

"You're all dying of radiation sickness and you want to get into
that place. And nobody smile, thank you."

I stood there with Nicholas Meyer on a hot summer day and I
thought, *This is it.* This is the guy who made the movie that's been
making me crazy, the movie I couldn't quite seem to understand,
the movie that to me, at least, seems more and more relevant every
day. Above us, the green canopy of trees tempered the heat. The gate
swung closed and I had stepped behind the walls, into the secret city.

Utopian Dreams

WHEN I TELL people we live in Fresno, California, now and then they raise an eyebrow. I like to mention that we have an underground arboretum. *Underground arboretum*, I'll repeat, hoping the contradiction of what I'm saying will suggest something about what I like about our new home. I like this place because, well, it's complicated.

We took our son to the underground arboretum, and I hoped he learned something, hoped he saw some of the beauty I saw. I wanted him to forget the possible nuclear power plant, the toxic air, the gang violence, and the unrelenting poverty in Fresno. I wanted him to forget the fires over the horizon, the earthquakes, and the missiles aimed at our state. Instead, I wanted him to remember Baldassare Forestiere and his underground arboretum.

Some days I dream of applying for a job there as a tour guide.

The place sits just off the ugly story that is Highway 99, and it looks like very little from the outside. Maybe just a patch of dirt, a few trees, and a battered old house. But inside the fence, down the holes, you find a tree-filled underground home, a "resort" that never really opened: skylights, cubbies, kitchens, closets, the kind of place that still makes me envious, still makes me want to move in tomorrow, taking up residence in one of the undeveloped caverns carved out of hardpan and stone.

Forestiere spent forty years digging there, dreaming of something just beyond his grasp. He saw something beneath the surface, a place where he could live and flourish, a place below and beyond the injuries and scars of the surface. Forestiere's utopian dream was a dream of ends that paid off in the means, the work, the process of digging, carving, and building—frantically building, burrowing like an animal rooting out his home.

He is my new hero—this man of the earth and the shovel.

ONE DAY, IN the midst of my childhood phase of atomic angst, my friends and my brother and I found a new paradise on the western edge of Lawrence. Giant pallets stacked with dusty red brick, destined for a development of town homes, spawned grand visions of forts, streets, and cities of stone.

We moved among the piles silently, knowingly, our eyes aglow with possibility, and with few words or plans we simply started building our homes, stacking and scrounging for scrap lumber. It must be primal and instinctual, this impulse to construct. We'd just started building our first walls, laying out the first foundations of a new civilization, when dusk settled. We gathered before parting for home, these short-legged soldiers of the new millennium, buzzing with excitement.

The landscape of the evening, the weekend, the near future, appeared where only a field of weeds and thistle once stood. If there was value in suburban sprawl, it was in its transformative zeal, its push to remake and change the landscape. Our sprawl was innocent enough, miniaturized and simple, harmlessly strange. When we drifted home after dark, the walls of a small brick city had begun to rise from blank space. Civilization had spread where there had once been emptiness. A city from nothing.

In the morning, after Orion Samuelson's *U.S. Farm Report* and *Super Friends*, we made excuses to extricate ourselves from our families and return to the project. We gathered and started building again, feverishly and furiously. Not all the kids came back. Matt and I returned. Karl W. too, Jeff F. and Ronnie O. Boys with the drive and dream to build something new—the same boys who would hopefully help me fight off the Russians one day.

We constructed four-foot walls with windows and doorways and laid sheets of plywood over the top. We built brick mansions with verandas and porches, guesthouses and parking spots. We built cottages and cabins. We planned out sidewalks and gardens and crafted deck chairs from bricks and scrap wood. We built parks and playgrounds—all the stuff that kids need to survive.

Our own little utopia felt so permanent, so real, so solid—even if we were aware of its fragility. Pretty quickly the city began to divide itself aesthetically. Some built lazy structures where I wouldn't house a dog. My Taj Mahal, on the other hand, included a curved wall and a crudely arched doorway, small partitions for rooms, and even a lounge chair made from a warped piece of plywood.

In an attempt to acknowledge the more adult concerns of a new civilization—things like laws, courts, and incarceration—we built a town jail, an imposing brick structure that also happened to be the tallest in town and the one building that all of us teamed up to build, the only real group effort in our little utopia.

"So what gets you in jail?" Matt asked.

"Laws and stuff," I said.

"Like what?"

"I don't know. We'll figure that out later."

Nobody was quite sure how one ended up in the town jail, but all of us agreed that it was not a pleasant place to be, especially during the heat of the day, when we imagined it must get unbearably hot and stinky and full of biting bugs and perhaps even poisonous copperhead snakes. We didn't know why, exactly, we needed a jail, but we knew it was an important part of any community. By the end of Saturday, when our parents emerged from the brush and dragged us home, we had built something special.

RECENTLY, MY SON and I drove to the craft store in Fresno and bought 1,000 popsicle sticks for a project. We bought 1,000 because it was cheaper than buying 300, and we figured we'd have plenty of raw material for future developments.

We took the sticks home and plugged in the hot glue gun. We started building, not with any real grand plan in mind. We could have built animals or stars or pinwheels or something. But we built houses. It was probably my fault. I tried not to control or guide him too much. Soon enough, we had structures on stilts with bridges between them, and the first two were a jail and a "Sherif" office. Those were his choices, his words.

We had the beginnings of our own community—fully equipped to deal with crime and punishment. Just like our little red brick village when I was a kid.

Back then, after our first day of real progress in Alvamar, I dreamed of our red brick city and couldn't wait to return. We went back after church the next day, and the city still stood tall. Other kids gathered and we spent our last few hours of fantasy lounging around our suburban homes, pretending to smoke cigars and drink beer, pretending to yell at our invisible kids.

We all knew that tomorrow morning we would board the bus for school and the workmen would show up. We knew they would knock down our town, flattening our suburban dreams to build bigger ones—a tiny sort of apocalypse. We knew our red brick utopia would give way to someone else's living room, dining room, veranda, front porch, and garden of the future. We knew our dreams would become a family's home. We knew all of this but we didn't speak of it. It was Sunday, the day of rest, the weekend almost over. We listened to the crickets crank up in the brush and the chemical hum of the lone street lamp and we were silent and undeniably happy.

AT SCHOOL, MY dreams of survival didn't end completely. Nor did the disappointment. My apocalyptic drama was simply miniaturized. In the midst of a complicated home life and problems fitting in, I became a first-rate cardboard architect. I built model homes in my spare time. One week, perhaps inspired by our brick city, I convinced the other kids in my cluster of desks that we should build a city for our Matchbox and Hot Wheels cars—a new and glorious toy utopia.

I brought supplies and we built a miniature city from Dad's cigar boxes and the backs of Big Chief writing tablets. We were high-end builders, subcontracting solely for the Hot Wheels set. No Fisher-Price plastic crap in our neighborhood. No mistakes. We developed a sprawling and multileveled subdivision of flat-roofed White Owl cigar-box houses spread out over the terraced Formica landscape. It looked like a Spanish villa or a vacation retreat in the South of France. It looked like something from a different world, a better world. We were industrious, ambitious, and still learning our multiplication tables.

Soon a new city had risen from the flat planes of our desks. Reinforced cardboard ramps and tunnels connected the short and taller desks. Paper-clip streetlamps lit the neighborhood. We all drove Corvettes, Camaros, and other impractical hot rods. We rolled around in Jeeps and yellow stock cars plastered with Mountain Dew and Pennzoil labels. We parked their die-cast bodies in cigar-scented palaces. My sweet ride was a black Chevy van with red-and-orange flames, the closest thing to an SUV back then. But I also drove a white Lotus with a British flag on the hood, a car I like to think lent our little village a distinctly international flair. It was a village that blossomed into a community of dedicated car-loving suburbanites happily rolling along wide, well-lit boulevards. We had created our own little vacation spot, and every day we traveled someplace else in our minds, a safe place away from politics and fear.

While we were away for the weekend, safe at home, tucked in our child beds, the silent, silver-haired janitor who roamed the hall with a wide red dust mop descended upon our village. Without so much as a warning-siren signal, she tore our houses down, ripped through our town like an F5 tornado, and wiped everything away. In her wake, I could see myself in the shine of my desk.

On Monday we gathered around and mourned the loss of our homes and our dream town. Maybe you can picture the helicopter photos of storm-battered townspeople gathering after a tornado strike—only there was no rubble for us to sift through, no family pictures to hold up for cameras, no symbolic finds like a dead wife's watch, a photograph, or a precious juicy orange.

Our city was unceremoniously dumped into a plastic bag and heaved into the dumpster. Fortunately, we had all driven our Matchbox and Hot Wheels cars to our weekend homes. Otherwise the losses might have been even more catastrophic. Wordless and dumb with grief, we stood and wondered at the random violence of the janitor's storm, the tiny apocalypse that had befallen our town.

Fueled by innocent optimism or ignorant denial, we immediately began to rebuild—our hearts bursting with the nostalgia for paper houses taped together by hand, pencil-drawn patios, and imaginary vegetable gardens. We ignored any lingering fallout, all suggestion of future attack, but all week we watched the janitor roam the halls in a new light. She swung her bucket of sawdust ominously, dumping it on pools of kid vomit, and wielded her mop like a staff. She stomped around the school like a thunderstorm brewing. Friday came again and another Matchbox Town cardboard city stood tall again, towering higher than the original with double-decker box houses and complicated ramp systems. It was truly spectacular and golden. A phoenix to behold. Built to last.

On Friday I left a note:

Dear Janitor,
  Please don't tear down our city. We worked real hard to make it.
Mrs. Frakes says it's OK if we keep it. Thank you.
                                          —The Kids from Cluster 4

The weekend lasted forever. We wanted to believe in the goodness of
humanity, or, more specifically, the goodness of the janitor. We hoped
she had a heart or at least an appreciation for the imaginative industry
of a child. But when we returned to school on Monday, our desks were
scoured clean, our city destroyed all over again. There was nothing
left, no trace of our efforts, our dreams, and the chemical smell of
Comet cleanser lingered in the air. Utterly defeated. Crushed. Cursed.
Wiped away. We didn't ever bother to rebuild this time—our spirits
splintered, our suburban dreams diffused into wisps of nothing.

I still have trouble understanding the violence of this storm, and I
begin to imagine the janitor after hours, drooling over her destructive
work, her fingers punching down through the cardboard roofs, ripping them from their Scotch-tape moorings. She yanked and pulled
and dropped it all in the garbage. She enjoyed the destruction. And
suddenly, in the midst of my imagining, I feel sorry for her.

Now I see her at home alone, struggling to paint by numbers,
anguishing over a rickety popsicle-stick castle. I see her knitting
pathetic four-fingered gloves for children she never had, sweaters with
tiny neck holes, and uncomfortable socks. I see her as a child, building
teetering, awkward Lincoln Log shacks and Tinker Toy contraptions
that never quite worked. I see her tiny little life, her face illuminated
by the electric blue glow of the television, her silvery hair cropped
short and her wide smudged eyeglasses. I smell the cheap TV dinners
in tin trays with a mushy peach cobbler for dessert. I conjure up a
character who is more sympathetic. Maybe she resented us for our
architecture, our ambition, and our imagination. Maybe she envied
our innocent sprawl. Maybe she just took her job too seriously. Maybe
she was a messenger from the future, warning us of the apocalypse.
We didn't know. We were simple boys—not much different from my
own son and his friends—vessels of developing hubris and dreams,
and we could not be blamed for the desire to create in the face of certain death. We could not be blamed for our hope, however small, of a
new and better world than the one we inherited.

DAHLBERG VARIATION: Letter to the Author

Dear Steve Church,

Testing. Testing. Steve-O. Good to hear from you. You're not far from me now, heh? You could visit me some time, bring some gifts, things from the outside world. I'm in my own hole now. You know, here in the desert you can't trust anyone. Been down for almost twenty years. Feels like a hundred. I built my underground home just like ones I designed when I was kid. I kept the drawings stuffed in my desk drawers all those years, and I retrieved them after the blast, when we emerged from the cellar. I brought them to life. Skylights and everything. Lots of white cabinets and walls and my very own bunker, a sort of inner sanctum. Twelve by twelve with twelve-inch concrete-block walls, steel-plated, insulated, air-conditioned with its own generator and water system. Floor vaults packed to the gills with canned food and MREs. Quite a feat of engineering. There's a wood shack on the surface, a little carport, some cacti and ocotillos. That's where my editorial intern works, transcribing my scrawl into typeface . . . I know she changes words, plays with diction, mixes up my sentences, and rearranges my thoughts before she sends out these letters. What can I say? I need her help. I don't trust computers. Too many viruses, too many ways for them to track me. I don't type my personal correspondence. And my handwriting is nearly illegible . . . Look. Here's the truth. She knows my work. She understands me. What can I say? I can't fucking see half the time. My work needs a lot of editing, shaping, carving, dissecting. It needs a guiding hand . . . Christ, man, she doesn't stop. She's always on top of me, always hassling me for pages. "Keep 'em coming, Danny." She calls me Danny. I like that. She won't let me rest. But I know she'll fuck me. I mean, I know she'll leave someday. It's not what you're thinking. They all leave. They can't take it. They're weak. They're not ready for the apocalypse. They haven't found it yet. I'm just trying to help them understand the end of the world. This is an apprenticeship, working for me. I'm teaching them about production, about meeting the end with pages and pages of other worlds. I'm teaching them about the kinds of sacrifices you have to be willing to make for your art, for the effort to understand our apocalyptic legacy. It's really that simple. But they don't appreciate it after a while. They think it's an act or something, that I'll grow tired of talking about the end, but I can't. It's something I carry with me—the movie, the blast, the blindness. Just don't ever give yourself completely to a movie. OK, Steve? You hear me. Look at the light. It changes you. It will change you . . . Next thing you know, you'll be bringing a fucking child into this world. Good god, how selfish is that? I mean, think about the sort of future you're giving him. Remember, Steve, as you said in your last letter, "It's not a matter of if but when there will be a nuclear attack on American soil." (As if I didn't know that!) Why not your soil? You better hope lightning doesn't strike twice. You're due for a meteorite impact, probably a hurricane too, maybe an earthquake. Could be a tornado too. You just moved from one target town to another, didn't you? Nice . . . OK, so I'm waiting for another letter from you, maybe a visit, a postcard, a symbolic gift. We'll talk about that. I'll need to check into some deadlines I have coming up. You say hello to your wife for me, OK? Good luck with that kind of commitment. I couldn't do it. I've got too much to lose. I can't drag myself out of the past, through the days after without facing the fallout.

Peas.

Danny Dahlberg
Sedona, Arizona

Dog Tags

NICHOLAS MEYER DIDN'T destroy my hometown, but he did remake it for me, and now I was inside his world. I followed him through a door affixed with a plaque that read 221B Baker St., Sherlock Holmes's address, and I stifled a yelp of recognition. Along with my comic books and cartoon obsessions as a boy, I also dearly loved the Sherlock Holmes mysteries—where the crusty and eccentric detective discerns great meaning from the tiniest details—and I'd read most of the best-selling Holmes novel *The Seven-Per-Cent Solution*, penned by Meyer himself, before driving down from Fresno.

We passed through what appeared to be some sort of breezeway or outbuilding that opened into a large central courtyard, and I was reminded of a Spanish villa, something I'd never actually seen except maybe in a movie somewhere.

I wanted to stop, look up and around, just take it all in and gawk at the spread. I didn't want to be so obvious about checking out his home and searching for clues, but at heart I was still a kid from Kansas who felt unsettled around so much wealth. Los Angeles felt like another world to me—a modern day Technicolor Oz—a world very far away from Kansas.

To my left stretched a long shimmering blue pool. Massive purple and white beach balls floated on the surface like planets, and two women in bikinis, dark sunglasses, and floppy hats reclined in wooden deckchairs. Drinks sweated next to them on small tables. They each lifted an arm and waved at me in a strange, synchronized kind of greeting. A huge Bernese mountain dog ambled away from us and flopped down on the pavement, closer to the women. He didn't really seem to notice me.

WE MADE OUR way inside, past a floor-to-ceiling bookshelf crammed with DVDs, and sat down in his kitchen for a moment.

Meyer made me an iced coffee. As we drank, he told me that he was born in 1945 and grew up in Manhattan. Like my parents, he grew up with the bomb. He feared nuclear attacks by the Russians and recalled the infamous duck-and-cover public service filmstrips they showed to American schoolchildren.

"It was scary stuff," he said as he took a sip of coffee and peered at me over his glass. "I wore dog tags."

I gulped. "Dog tags?" I asked. I'd never heard of anything like this.

"Sure. So they could identify my body if they found it in the rubble," he said and stood up, turning away from me and walking across the room.

I was just about to ask whether these dog tags were issued by his school or his parents or some other authority when Meyer announced that he had to make a quick phone call. He picked up the phone and turned his back to me.

I sat in his kitchen and thought to myself, *Dog tags?* Soldiers wear dog tags. They didn't issue dog tags to us in the '80s, but they could have, I supposed. I couldn't really imagine my parents hanging such things on me. It would be too pessimistic, too fatalistic, too real. I wondered if Meyer still had his dog tags somewhere, hidden away in a safe or his dresser drawer.

From another room somewhere, I heard the sound of piano music, the tinkling of keys. Meyer's daughter was in the middle of a piano lesson at the time. She was good too, clearly a child who practiced her art, a child with discipline. I doubted that she was wearing dog tags, but it was possible.

As he talked on the phone, I thought about the fact that Meyer and I were both raising children in this world, perhaps grappling with some of the same questions and challenges as parents. But then again, he was old enough to be my father, and he had grown children too. Meyer was an expert, a veteran of these battles. I was a newbie, a rookie, a greenie; but I also had a half-brother who was just a couple of years older than Meyer's daughter. And this meant the three of us—Meyer, my father, and I—were all raising kids who could be in the same school together, kids who could be ducking and covering together, crowded in the hallways with their heads between their knees.

I wondered if Meyer still worried about nuclear war. I wondered if his daughter had internalized some of that fear, like my son had. He worries now about a nuclear power plant in the neighborhood. Does Meyer's daughter ask the same sorts of questions?

One day I found a drawing in my son's school backpack featuring screaming yellow-faced stick figures, a pool of blue and green slime, and the caption *I will cry to keep away radiation from people*.

Meyer hung up the phone, but I didn't have time to ask about his children or family, or the lessons he teaches them, no time to ask whether he still kept his dog tags or whether his daughter dreamed of mutants and mutually assured destruction. We were off again, cruising through sprawling rooms filled with fine furniture and antiques. He moved fast and I followed, eager to see where this trip might lead.

MEYER'S STUDY WAS painted dark green and the walls covered with art and books. A toy train track wound its way around the perimeter, but the train itself sat dormant in the corner, collecting dust. Meyer invited me to sit on one of two love-seat couches that faced each other, separated only by about three feet of space, most of which was dominated by a long, narrow coffee table. I couldn't quite fit my legs between the couch and the table, so I had to sit at kind of an angle. I tried not to put my feet on his table. He sat barefoot with his feet up on the sofa. He asked if I wanted to take some notes or anything. He clearly seemed accustomed to giving interviews, probably interviews about this very topic—the cultural and historical legacy of *The Day After*. But I also wanted him to tell me about the symbolic meaning of Kansas, and Lawrence in particular. I wanted to learn.

As we settled in, I noticed a framed photograph on a side table. I leaned in to take a closer look and saw a woman dressed like Dorothy from *The Wizard of Oz*. She posed in front of a fake horse stall, holding a red basket on her arm, and she was surrounded by bright yellow hay.

Before I could ask about the woman or anything else, Meyer began delivering what amounted to a monologue on the legacy of his movie. I just sat back and listened for a while. Like the film he made, Meyer is enigmatic and paradoxical. He's a Sherlock Holmes scholar, a hero to Trekkies the world over, a sailor, a father, a writer, a director, a producer, and a graduate of the University of Iowa, a place for which he still had fond memories.

"So why was the movie set in Lawrence, Kansas?" I asked when I found an opening.

He waited, considering the question, and gave me a look. I gulped, hoping I hadn't offended him in some way.

"Lawrence reminded me a lot of Iowa City," he said. "I liked it."

"Was it something about Kansas as a state? I mean, did Kansas mean something?"

Meyer just kind of looked at me funny.

"I don't know about any of that," he said, and an awkward silence settled over the room. I felt defeated.

I pointed at the picture on the table. "Your wife?" I asked, taking a gamble. I couldn't see it clearly. It could have been an older daughter in the picture. I thought perhaps I crossed a line.

Suddenly Meyer's face brightened and the mood lifted a bit. I relaxed and sat back in the love seat. He confirmed that it was, in fact, his wife dressed up for Halloween as Dorothy. Though not directly addressing my question on the meaning of Kansas, he revealed to me that he was a huge *Wizard of Oz* nut when he was a kid and that, to this day, he and his sister spoke in a kind of secret code by quoting lines from the movie back and forth to each other. The movie was their lingua franca, their private language and a shared story.

Somehow I knew it. I knew that Meyer had grown up in Kansas too.

As he talked, the director's hands punctuated his sentences with sharp stabs from his fingers and twirling flourishes—almost more conductor than director or interview subject. His eyes seemed to bore holes into my skull, leaving me dumbfounded and awestruck. He had a little bit of Svengali in him, a certain magnetism I could feel. I found myself sitting silently and listening to him talk about his movie and the larger world, and I could have kicked my shoes off and stayed all day. I just wanted him to fill in the gaps, the spaces and silences in the story, the lines I never imagined, and I wanted him to map out the intersections where it all comes together.

6

DAHLBERG VARIATION: Letter to the Author

Dear Steve,

   I understand your compulsion to talk about Oz and Baum and poor little Dorothy. I know you think Meyer is going to answer all your questions, that he's going to make it all make sense. But you can't forget the specific history, the true stuff. The facts of Lawrence as apocalyptic landscape. Don't forget the quotes from Rev. Fisher. The sack-cloth. The ashes. The degraded tribes. The city shorn of its beauty and sons. The reference to the mythical phoenix, the thunderbirds. Have you thought about this? It's there, man. The apocalyptic legacy, the history. People underestimate the horror. Can you imagine the terror? . . . They didn't call it Bleeding Kansas for nothing. See, this is what comes before. This is what lays the groundwork. The Reverend Fisher. His words . . . And they are so grandiose. Overwrought. Like a pulpit speech, a sermon. But where was Rev. Fisher during the carnage on that morning in 1863? What did he do for those defenseless boys? He didn't give them guns and send them into the woods. He didn't hide them in his cellar. In the end, all he offered were words. I can't find him in the pictures, can't see him in other stories. But I can imagine him, huddled in his root cellar, sequestered in the parsonage, quivering from the fear. He had sense enough to stay inside, still in his bedclothes. He's got a tablet, a charcoal pencil, and he's already begun chronicling, knowing that this will make a great sermon later, knowing that he can use this to motivate people, to etch his name into the history books . . . Too cynical? . . . You're right. I know. But this should be used as some kind of foreshadowing for things to come. Fisher for you is one of the first storytellers of the end, one of the first re-creators of the old story. Fisher, Baum, Meyer . . . Maybe Fisher was more heroic, more tragic vessel. Right. I can see this too. I can imagine him, white bed robe, skullcap draped over his shoulder, arms held up to the sky, beseeching the Lord to come to the aid of Lawrence, to save them from the carnage. I can see Quantrill himself, stinking of sweat and fire smoke, his pants spattered with blood. He stops his horse in front of the Reverend's parsonage, dismounts, and raises his sword. As the Reverend drops to his knees, wailing and chanting Bible verses, Quantrill pauses, steps forward, grabs him by the shirt cloth, drags him to his feet, presses his foul whiskered face into the Reverend's. He tells him not to forget what he has seen, tells him that William Quantrill did this, William Quantrill slaughtered the sons of Lawrence.

This Rev. Fisher. He gets a lot of quotes, all the most melodramatic lines. But there had to be other witnesses, other stories more personal and full of real pain, images of fathers dying in the arms of their wives and children, blood spilling on the wooden porch, the squirmy white-and-red mess of guts, the vacant look and oddly clean bullet wound in a skull . . . the anger of a child left behind. Where are the boys? Where is the boy-child of Daniel, the kid hidden in the basement with his mother and sister? Perhaps he emerged after the noise stopped. Perhaps he found his father dead in the street, defenseless as Jim Dahlberg. Perhaps he pulled him out of the street, up onto the porch steps and held his head in his lap and dabbed at his father's gaping wounds with his shirtsleeves— like dropping a Kleenex into a puddle.

This is why my protagonist is a survivor, a blind boy riddled with guilt, because he lived while his father and his older brother died in the apoca- lypse, the brother who wouldn't stay behind, down in the basement, the brother who rushed off to his own death, the same one they would find piled up with others . . . He has these visions of the future. Prophetic sorts of stuff. Like Tiresias. This is the sort of narrator a good story needs, the sort of new hero of the apocalypse, a boy who can lead other children into the future. Children against the end. Children against the enemy within. Children are the true soldiers of the imagination, the only ones capable of picturing a better world. That's what you're stuck with. That's the truth.

Winged monkeys and gingham.

Danny Dahlberg

Sedona, Arizona

7

Second Summit

At first, after the divorce, Mom moved out and into in a tiny two-bedroom garden-level apartment on 9th Street, in a complex dominated mostly by college students and single working people. Matt and I shared a room with a tiny window. For a while we slept on air mattresses. After a few months there, Mom moved into a small yellow house a block from our school and three blocks from Dad's house. The divorce wasn't finalized yet, but you could tell that she was done with Dad. She'd applied to a master's program at the university and would stay up late after work, tapping away on an old word processor that looked like a massive typewriter with a tiny one-line screen.

Dad tried to adapt too, but we could tell that he wasn't quite done with being married to Mom, or at least the idea of it. When she rented the yellow house closer to Dad's, it made it easier for us to make the trip back and forth.

It also made it easier for Dad to do drive-bys.

Dad often made a point of driving by Mom's house. It didn't matter that there were numerous ways to avoid doing this. It didn't matter if we were heading in the opposite direction. He did it anyway. Enough that it got to where I felt anxious every time we left the house, climbed in the car, and pulled out of the driveway.

Dad would slow the car as he passed Mom's house and he'd stare out the window. He'd never say a word. He'd just drive past slowly, confirming something, and turn his chin back to the street, saying little to us. He didn't have to. We knew Dad was barely holding it together, barely keeping his head above water. He was torn up pretty bad and we saw it in these brief but telling moments, these small glimpses at the rubble of a divorce. Most of the time he kept the emotion of it all buried in a vault somewhere deep inside. Only rarely did he let it out.

Once when he picked us up from school for our half of the week

with him, I plopped down in the front seat of his car, barely acknowl-
edging him, and immediately began complaining about a small hole
in the seam of my Polo shirtsleeve, right where it attaches to the
shoulder. I went on and on about how I need new clothes and how I
just got this shirt and now it was already falling apart.

Dad turned and looked at me. He said, "You mean this little hole,"
and poked his finger into it.

"Yeah," I responded indignantly.

"This one?" he asked and hooked his finger through the hole.

"Yeah," I said, looking at him cautiously.

Dad grinned, yanked hard, and ripped the sleeve off my shirt.

"Now *that's* a hole," he said.

And while I was momentarily traumatized by the destruction of
my Polo shirt, I knew that *he* knew what he was talking about when
it came to recognizing important holes in your life. His business had
collapsed, spiraling us into massive debt, and his wife had left him. A
hole had opened up before us—a great gaping chasm—and it would
take cooperation for all of us to avoid falling in even further. It would
take a suspension of the cynicism I felt and perhaps even a small
degree of hope. This was hard for me. But I tried. I learned to adapt
and dance around the impact.

At Dad's house, things were different. He bought groceries in bulk—
a lot of stuff we could cook in the microwave—and kept a tower of
twelve-packs of soda in the garage. The evergreen hedges out front
grew largely unchecked, looking like nappy Afros, and he had to chain
the porch chairs to a post to keep the frat boys from stealing them.
The front yard had a dirt oval carved into the grass where we rode our
motorcycles, and the grass was often yellow and brittle to the touch.
On one side of the house an apple tree dropped forgotten fruit.

One day my friend Andy P. and I grabbed a can of silver spray paint
from the garage and crept around the house, following the sweet stink
of rotting apples and the low humming buzz of bees.

I stepped up close to the apples and sprayed a thick coat of paint
over several of them. All the bees rose up, but a few of them moved
slower than the others. They sputtered, dodged, dipped, and weaved
around like drunks. They hovered for a moment, their silver bodies whizzing over the stinking fruit, floating in the dappled sunlight,
before bobbing and zipping off to die.

AT SOME POINT, in the midst of the recent rubble, someone, some kind of authority, decided my family needed to get together and talk about things. Maybe a judge? Talk is what we needed. More talking. I think the adults were frightened. So we had to go and talk to someone. A professional talker. Someone who gets paid to break the silence. I wasn't looking forward to our second summit as a splintered family.

The therapist's office was located at the mental health center, a building near the hospital that, because of its name, I'd always imagined was teeming with lunatics in straitjackets. It was an imposing edifice of brick and glass that looked like a hospital or a jail. We followed Mom into a side door, still hoping for some miracle of scheduling, dreaming that the therapist was busy restraining one of the many lunatics that must be kept upstairs. No such luck. The interior was dark and poorly lit, covered with muted orange carpet and beige office furniture. Potted plants hung from hooks. Boxy fluorescent lights buzzed overhead. Dad waited in the lobby. He didn't look particularly happy to be there either, but he smiled at Matt and me.

"Hey, guys," he said, and we mumbled greetings in return.

He barely looked at Mom.

We all waited for a few minutes in the lobby, milling around stiffly and silently. The therapist appeared from down the hall. He seemed to be the only other person in the building, and I suddenly wanted the halls to be teeming with the insane and emotionally disturbed. I wanted to see nurses in white jackets, a whole waiting room filled with patients. This was all just a bit too weird.

The therapist wore a brownish sweater and green slacks, and he had wispy feathered dirty-blond hair. He shook Dad's hand first, smiling, and then greeted the rest of us grimly and seriously. We followed him down the hall to his office. I didn't know what to expect, but a couch sat against one wall and there were several mustard-colored chairs. Matt and I sat together on the couch, Mom and Dad in chairs on opposite sides of us, and the therapist directly in front of the couch in another chair. The couch was sort of low-slung, so Matt and I sat below the level of the adults.

"Shall we begin?" the therapist asked, looking first to Dad and then the rest of us.

But I didn't get the feeling that I had a choice in the matter.

Mom shifted nervously, staring at the carpet.

The therapist told us that we were there to talk about our feelings surrounding the divorce, that the goal was to communicate openly and honestly about what we thought. It was important that *we*—Matt and I—talk about what's going on inside.

"You have to let the emotions out and share your feelings," the therapist said.

This is what they said about *The Day After* and our fears of a nuclear apocalypse, and something Matt and I heard constantly from adults. It was a common refrain, and pretty ironic considering it came from a generation known for silence and suppression of emotion. To me it felt like an obvious attempt to control what we were thinking and feeling. If they could get my thoughts out, they could define them, shape them, and change them. I didn't want that happen. I just wanted to keep everything to myself and let them worry and squirm. I knew I should put my best face forward for the therapist. But I didn't care.

In a world that felt out of control, my internal thoughts and dreams were some of the only things I could control. Silence was my power and imagination my best defense, but when you just sit quietly and boil with fantasy, adults tend to think you'll inevitably explode. They could hear us *tick-tick-tick*ing with concussive force. Few things frightened adults more than silent, angst-ridden children—perhaps because they knew that our raw, pink, untarnished minds were always dancing along the line between chaos and normalcy. We were just smart enough to be dangerous.

Matt and I talked to each other, but it was mostly about how adults just wouldn't leave us alone, that they suddenly cared *soooo* much about our feelings when, before all this end-of-the-world shit, they often ignored us. But they really didn't understand. It wasn't that easy. If we had feelings we could identify, we couldn't name them and define them. We didn't know how to speak the language of adults, didn't know about things like anxiety or depression. We didn't know our lines.

The therapist droned on and on about how important it was for us to talk and share and be honest, and you could tell he'd been prompted to do this, that Dad or Mom—or both of them, and maybe the school psychologist too—had asked him to get us to talk and open up and let our feelings out.

So then he said to me, "I want you to start by talking about your parents' divorce and how that makes you feel. How do you *feeeeel* about your mom moving out?"

My brain began to buzz and ache. The orange colors in the room pulsed and throbbed and a dull ringing rose up in the back of my ears. A macramé tree on the wall sprouted new limbs and leaves and stretched its roots down at me. I felt like the therapist was holding a match to my fuse, pouring gas on the embers.

Mom cringed and covered her face, blotting tears with a tissue. Dad seemed uncomfortable too. He didn't really want this. I barely said a word and the therapist kept asking questions until both Matt and I were reduced to spasms of crying and made valiant but ill-fated efforts to express ourselves. The therapist seemed to bloat out and up like a brown toad. His presence filled up the room and I slowly realized that this had little do with us.

He just kept going, opening his mouth, croaking and burping. He wanted us to be angry about the divorce. He wanted us to feel traumatized. But we had been angry. We had done that already, and then we had to make a choice: stay that way, or adapt to the new territory of forgiveness and acceptance.

But if he kept pushing me, I knew things could get ugly.

I'd spin my other face around, channel the Hulk and transform before their eyes into a raging green beast, muscles ripping through my Toughskin jeans, bursting out of my Izod shirt, and a window-rattling roar emanating from deep within my diaphragm. I'd snort at the therapist and smash his desk with a mighty hand chop, grab him by the torso and pop his head off with my thumb like he was a dandelion weed. Then I'd throw a chair through the window, sending bright shards out into the day, and spring from that office with Matt, leaving our parents slack-jawed and awestruck at the power of my silence untethered, unleashed, and clearly underappreciated.

Instead, I shrank inside myself and mumbled a few answers that I thought the therapist might want to hear. Matt fell completely mute and seemed to leave the room entirely, even though he sat right next to me. Mom couldn't get a word in edgewise and fidgeted nervously in her seat, clearly wanting to be out of there as badly as I did. Dad's faced twisted around like someone was pinching him the whole time or like he had stomach cramps. The whole meeting rapidly deteriorated, and I realized that this second summit of sorts, this forced meeting, would do little to end the small wars in the new land of family. We would never be together again. I knew this. I just didn't see the need to talk about it.

DR. RICHARD GIST is a psychologist who works with the Kansas City Fire Department (and other organizations), and he is an outspoken critic of the sort of trauma debriefing they conducted on kids after *The Day After* was telecast, and, more recently, the therapy conducted on survivors and victims of both 9/11 and Hurricane Katrina.

He is fond of saying that "we learn a lot more about coping with fear from our grandmas than from graduate school," and he's argued with some success that the sort of forced talk therapy we tend to foist on trauma survivors can actually cause more harm than good, can even make people *more* traumatized and fearful.

Dialogue isn't always a good thing. My grandma didn't play basketball, but I think she would have understood. She would have clutched me to her chest and talked to me about collectible plates or pinochle or the waltz she was writing for her electric organ.

Dr. Gist apparently came to his professional epiphany while working to deal with the loss of six Kansas City firefighters in an explosion in the early '80s. He also worked on the 1981 Hyatt Regency skywalk collapse in Kansas City—an event I remember vividly because some of my friends' parents were there when it happened. He decries what he calls the "outsourcing of compassion" to poorly trained psychotherapists who are ill-equipped to deal with the variation of responses to trauma and disaster, and he suggests that they, in fact, magnify the trauma through their tactics of aggressive intervention and talk therapy.

What struck me most about Dr. Gist's ideas in connection to *The Day After* was that we had experienced the first wave of a new kind of psychotherapy, a new level of response to the influence of television. With all the talk in our schools and the therapists visiting our classes, we had effectively been part of an experiment in trauma debriefing and were subjected to the sort of talk pressure that Vietnam vets and other trauma survivors experienced. The obvious difference being, of course, that we had survived not a real war . . . but a TV movie.

We were asked repeatedly to give voice to our fears, to talk about the movie and how it made us feel. But there always seemed to be one answer they were looking for. They seemed to be cuing us to simply say:

I'm scared out of my mind.

I'm filled with feelings of hopelessness and despair.

I'm wrought with anxiety for our human condition.

The goal seemed to be not to ease fears but to generate them. For the most part, I was happy to oblige. I was scared to death of the apocalypse. But this was a *fictional* apocalypse, not an actual traumatic event. It was a TV movie. It was a fake, a fabrication. How do you feel real trauma about a television show? Is it different if it's a show about your town, starring people you know?

The reactions to this manufactured trauma were as unique and varied as the kids who shared them. Some kids like me *were* scared out of their minds. Some kids felt hopelessness and despair. Some were worked up with anxiety. Other kids thought it was boring or melodramatic. Still others found it as momentarily compelling and transiently traumatic as a car wreck on the side of the highway. Some of them just thought it cool to see Kansas City get totally wasted by bombs. For many children, the manufactured responses expected of them were just as confusing and alienating as the manufactured trauma.

The movie was supposed to change the world. It was supposed to make a difference—at least in the long term. Perhaps its power is something that lingers, buried underground, and which resurfaces years later in unexpected forms, voices, and characters. Perhaps it's simply another voice in a post-apocalyptic dialogue—a kind of back-and-forth between hope and despair that has always characterized such stories. Or maybe it's something more elusive and transient, something silver and buzzing that rises up from the rot and floats away.

New Dawn

IT IS OCTOBER 1984 now, a month or more since the Russian invasion of America, and the harsh nip of winter has descended on the High Plains and mountains of the mythic West. A light dusting of snow covers the ground. The deer have begun to descend from the hills, searching for green shoots of food. Somewhere out there the Wolverines remain restless and hungry for vengeance.

A Russian tank crew pulls up to a lonely rural gas station, parking next to the pumps. The commander tells the soldiers to fill it up, and as they climb down a pretty girl rides up on a bicycle with a basket on the back. Just an innocent girl. Like something you've seen in a Vietnam War movie. A girl on a bicycle with a basket of goodies—like Red Riding Hood off to see her granny—and you just don't ask why she would be riding a bicycle up to an isolated gas station.

One of the wolfish young soldiers grabs her, saying, "Hey, pretty girl—you be my girlfriend," as she struggles to get away. The tank commander, wearing a light-blue beret, orders them to take her basket and forget about her. One of the soldiers tosses the basket up to the commander and he drops it in the tank, never once looking inside.

As the girl frees herself and starts walking away, the bomb goes off. Smoke and flame leap out of the tank, and she runs now. She runs away, off into the field, and the surviving Russians chase after her . . . and this is where I see myself. This is where I imagine myself in the story. This is the best scene.

She runs, stumbling out into the frozen field, her arms pinwheeling around, and we already know that she and her sister have probably been raped by Russian soldiers. She runs and I want to help. I want to reach out and pull her to safety. And just when it seems like she's not going to get away, just when all seems lost, the prairie cracks, splits its skin, and doors open.

The Wolverines rise up from buried bunkers and mow down the

pursuing soldiers with sprays of automatic gunfire, and I want to cheer. I want to raise my rifle too and shout "Wolverines!" at the top of my lungs, because I too believe that I could mount a similar defense of my family and my community.

I knew that I could take my Remington twelve-gauge, my .22 rifle, my Dad's Marlin, and the sawed-off shotgun he keeps in the gun cabinet. I could take the Bowie knife, the billy club, and all the bullets I could carry. I could try to make it out to Clinton Reservoir, to the deep woods there, but the river was my backup plan.

Andy P. and his brother, Adam, could come too. They were pretty good about survival stuff and they'd keep me laughing. My brother Matt could come too, because you can't leave your brother behind in these stories, and because Matt's a better shot than me, more fearless. He'd be one to drink the deer blood, just like C. Thomas Howell. Maybe Ronnie O. too, but there were others who just wouldn't make it, boys who would be a liability in the war against the Russians—boys who were pampered and coddled by their mothers, ignored by their fathers, boys who would swallow a commie bug and lead them right to us. Then we'd have to kill him. We'd call ourselves the Lions of Lawrence and we'd make brazen daytime raids on Russian convoys and tank crews. We'd catch them crossing bridges and blow them up. We'd drop grenades in their tanks and barracks. We'd send a girl on a bicycle with a bomb in her basket and we'd rise from the prairie like ghosts, like angry spirits, and we'd destroy them all.

Times would be hard. News of the war and the wider world would be hard to come by, delivered only through coded messages on Russian-controlled radio stations, maybe the occasional underground signal, but we would learn of Free America, the safe zones, and the new order of things. We would try to cling to our humanity, our sense of common decency and teamwork. We would try not to turn on each other and become like the enemy. We would prove that we are better, that the American character cannot be beaten, and if we had to witness the execution-style slaughter of our fathers at a gravel pit, we would not forget. We would not cry and we would, above all else, seek vengeance for them.

Soon enough, I had a concrete plan of action for surviving World War III, and even if it was fantasy, it was the sort of fantasy I needed after *The Day After*.

IN THE SUMMER of 1984, just as the long winter ended, Hollywood offered us a different sort of response to the end of the world. Set in a small western town dubbed Calumet, Colorado, and actually filmed in Las Vegas, New Mexico, *Red Dawn* depicted the beginning of World War III, ushered in by a communist invasion of the United States combined with precision nuclear strikes on apparently *all* of our nuclear missile silos as well as several major U.S. cities—including Washington, D.C., Kansas City, and most of the Midwest, the bleeding heart of the country. Ground forces had been sent up through Mexico, through our unprotected border, to capture, control, and secure a perimeter. Denver was apparently an urban hell of starvation, lawlessness, and cannibalism. Paratroopers dropped from passenger planes (just like the Soviets in Afghanistan) and were dispatched to secure outposts like Calumet.

In addition to Russians in long coats and big hats, the movie was populated by cigar-smoking Latinos in snow-white camouflage—one of them, Commander Bella, played by *Super Fly* actor Ron O'Neal (yes, *Super Fly*). It's never entirely clear if Bella is Nicaraguan or Cuban, or if there are actually any non-Russian soldiers, but what is clear is the message of the movie about the dangers of communism in Central and South America—places like Grenada. In addition to its painfully transparent pro-gun, pro-military, and Republican agenda, the film is directed by a former Special Forces soldier and had more than one CIA advisor. In fact, it had CIA actors. The hard-ass Russian commander brought in to kill the Wolverines is actually played by former agency linguist William Smith.

Red Dawn was directed by John Milius, writer of the Joseph Conrad interpretation *Apocalypse Now,* one of my all-time favorite movies, a movie that still haunts me today. Milius is notorious for conducting press interviews with a loaded handgun on the table in front of him as an apparent show of his constitutionally protected right to bear arms. Or just because he feels more comfortable with a gun nearby. I don't know. He's kind of a scary guy—one of those warrior-poet types with an artistic and militaristic agenda.

After the initial strategic strike on the local high school, the communist invaders use the gun-registration lists to herd up the "troublemaking" locals and imprison them in a grim "re-education" camp located at the drive-in movie theater. Other people are allowed to walk the streets freely, shop, eat, and go about their lives—albeit under the watchful eye and sloganeering of the invaders. It's the gun owners who are eventually slaughtered on a high mesa.

Viewers followed the actions of a small group of high-school-age friends who manage to escape the attack on the school and flee to the hills with camping equipment, stockpiles of canned food, and a cache of sporting weapons—mostly rifles, shotguns, bows, arrows, and knives. The Cuban and Soviet invaders employ the tactic of overwhelming force, beginning with the shock and awe created by their initial attack. But the occupiers underestimate the resolve of the occupied people and their ability to mount an insurgent attack.

The story may sound familiar, but this is the mythical West. This is 1984. These boys have been trained in survival techniques by their gun-loving parents and grandparents. They know this landscape and they are fighting for pride, for family, and for vengeance. They are outnumbered and overpowered but still determined to chase the invading hoard from their homeland. It helps the message that the movie is populated with good-looking members of the '80s Brat Pack, making their warmongering much sexier.

We got super-hunk Patrick Swayze, cute but angry C. Thomas Howell, silent and awkward Charlie Sheen in his first movie role, and a young Jennifer Grey before her *Dirty Dancing* stint. Powers Boothe drops from the sky, a pilot shot down by Soviet invaders, and quickly seduces the mute and shell-shocked Lea Thompson of *Back to the Future* fame. Armed with their inferior "country" weapons and homemade explosives, they become a group to be feared, a tightly knit band of angst-filled teen heroes.

They call themselves the Wolverines, the name of their high school sports teams—a moniker they spray-paint on the burnt-out husks of tanks and jeeps they destroy. Soon the group launches an all-out insurgent offensive against the invading Cubans and Russians, complete with shoulder-fired rockets and more spray paint. They are fast-moving and aggressive attackers who strike unpredictably and with much ferocity. And they are just kids, not much older than my friends and I were when the movie came out.

We couldn't help but love them. They were so . . . like us, and they were leading a violent teenage rebellion against totalitarian authority figures. This was the best sort of escapist realistic fiction—the kind of fantasy that made us believe again that we could survive the apocalypse, that the sort of adaptation we needed was not genetic but emotional and psychological. It was about turning the pain and the fear into action.

The Wolverines—just a bunch of scared kids—turn their pain into an insurgent rebellion. After their fathers are gunned down by a firing squad, Swayze's character, Jed Eckert, tells them, "Don't you cry. Don't you ever cry again." And they don't. They grow up fast, turn the tide against the invading Cubans and Soviets with their brazen and daring guerrilla tactics, and free Calumet citizens from the reeducation camp at the drive-in movie theater where they broadcast propaganda on an eternal loop.

Of course the commies underestimate the determination and fearlessness of the rugged rebel fighters—just like they did in Afghanistan. These aren't your New York pansy lawyers fighting the occupiers. These aren't urban rich kids hiding out in their penthouses. These aren't the angst-ridden trust-funders from *St. Elmo's Fire*. These aren't even the embittered professor or doctor from *The Day After*. These are working class individualists, salt-of-the-earth boys and girls. These are football stars. These are the greasers of the rural '80s. We love them like we love ourselves. When they destroy a Soviet tank and bellow "Wolverines!", we all want to raise our voices too.

Red Dawn was the *Rocky* of post-apocalyptic movies. It had the emboldening effect of convincing legions of boys that, when push comes to shove, they could, in fact, defeat an invading horde of communists just as easily as they could beat the crap out of Apollo Creed, Clubber Lang, or that big steroid-addled Russian played by Dolph Lundgren. It was pure fantasy, but it was presented realistically and, because of this, it carried the seductive but ultimately false promise of empowerment.

I was not immune to the pull of such promises. There was something very comforting about *Red Dawn*. It's a movie about teamwork and friendship, survival in the face of overwhelming odds. It's a tale of adaptation and vengeance against injustice, a story of individualism triumphing over collectivism, a film about kids leading adults into a new post-apocalyptic world. It appealed to my sense of drama, destiny, and my own obsessive fears, as well as my predisposition to guns and the mountains.

After *The Day After*, conventional troops and parachutes felt comforting next to impersonal warheads and missiles falling from the sky. Though there were some nukes dropped in other places, that part of the story was kept mostly in the background, de-emphasized by the writers of *Red Dawn*. What mattered, what prevailed in this story, was the indomitable human spirit. And guns. Lots of guns.

The message was clear: Either we support the Republican administration's efforts to defeat the Soviets in the nuclear arms race, or communist paratroopers will drop from commercial airliners, land at school, shoot the children in the face, and herd all the gun owners into concentration camps. It was that simple.

Despite much hype and supposed controversy over the harsh reality of *Red Dawn*, the movie did not really challenge its audience. It was not complicated or dense, frantic or confusing. It comforted them, lulling them in the singsong metaphysics of post-apocalyptic fantasy. *Red Dawn* possessed all the escapist qualities of realistic fiction and provided for many Americans a kind of easy answer to the void of meaning cracked open by *The Day After*.

Beneficial Irrationality

I'M SURE IT was a no-brainer when Hollywood came calling on the mayor of a small college town in the early '80s. How could you say no? Estimates suggest that *The Day After* pumped almost one million dollars into the Lawrence economy. It was good business. But David Longhurst and other city leaders were also parents in 1982 when they made the decision to bring a fake apocalypse to town.

Today, though each man is old enough to *be* my father, Longhurst and Nicholas Meyer both have something in common with me, and with *my* father. We're all raising children of the next generation, the new American apocalypse—a story of the end that now feels more personal, more local and less global, but just as terrifying. We're all dads in this together, and I like to think that gives us all some common ground.

David Longhurst has young children, one still in school, just a few years older than my son. His first marriage collapsed around the same time as my parents' marriage, and judging by the age of his older children, Meyer probably faced a divorce in the '80s too. All three men remarried and had more kids in post–Cold War America—a profoundly hopeful act.

The divorce boom hit a lot of families in the '80s and obviously had an effect on the worldview of a generation. I wanted to ask these men if their divorces felt apocalyptic too, if it made their kids two-faced mutants—but I just couldn't quite do it.

I did have the guts to ask Longhurst if he had any reservations about *The Day After* coming to Lawrence in 1982. He responded matter-of-factly: "I had no reservations about the filming taking place in Lawrence or any negative impact that might have on the community."

That seems clear enough. *No reservations.*

After I prompted him with a few nosy questions about his background, Longhurst remembered that his own mother had been peripherally involved with the Manhattan Project at Los Alamos, New Mexico. He told me that she was a biologist who placed caged mice in the blast zone to test the effects of fallout.

I couldn't help but wonder what she might have thought about her son up there onstage arguing against nuclear proliferation while the children of Lawrence lived like mice trapped in the blast zone—or the fake blast zone.

Longhurst believed that, as troubling and absurd, even surreal as I'm suggesting *The Day After* might have been for Lawrence, the movie was a wake-up call the community, and perhaps even the world, desperately needed.

He did admit that my questions reminded him of the filmstrips he used to see in public school during the '50s and '60s—a mushroom cloud in the distance and kids scrambling beneath their desks in school to protect themselves.

He said, "This image, this stereotype, suggested that nuclear war is not 'the end of the world' and that we could certainly survive it—we needed only get underneath our desks and everything would be OK. *The Day After* shattered that stereotype."

It shattered the hope that defined his generation's relationship with the apocalypse. Even Nicholas Meyer's dog tags carried the promise of someone's survival, of being found at least and recognized. But by 1983, most kids my age believed that we would die sometime within the next ten years in an all-out nuclear war between Reagan and the Soviets. We believed this because that's what we were told. Repeatedly.

For me, and probably many others, *The Day After* confirmed my beliefs in the inevitability of the apocalypse and suggested it would be happening a lot sooner than we expected. However, many people in Lawrence, the mayor included—and many throughout the world—felt that this kind of collective suffering of a fake war might actually change minds and motivate masses. This optimism, though characteristic of the generation that believes it, was perhaps a bit misguided.

Longhurst himself admits, almost offhandedly, "Nothing significant changed as a result of the movie."

I don't want to believe this is true.

I got the feeling that, despite his statement, Longhurst would, like Nicholas Meyer, describe his experience with the movie as one of the most important things he ever did. It was probably one of his greatest challenges—one of his true shining moments—as a mayor. It gave him and the city of Lawrence a stage—just like a real tragedy. It's a shame, perhaps, that the only way for us to be heard was to destroy ourselves onstage, in a public performance of collective immolation.

I WONDERED IF someone like Nathan Berg, an extra in the movie but a kid with some acting experience already, would have a similar feeling about the impact of *The Day After*. I was hoping he could help me understand the artistic resonance of the film. Today, Nathan appears to have fully recovered from the apocalypse.

Nathan now holds a Ph.D. in economics and focuses his research and writing in *psychological* economics. When he isn't playing his guitar and touring with his band, the Halliburtons, he teaches, researches, and publishes papers on (among other really smart-sounding subjects) the phenomena of "beneficial irrationality" as it applies to the world financial markets.

Beneficial irrationality.

I really liked the ring of that. Despite the fact that I didn't know exactly what it meant, it just seemed to legitimize so much of my obsession with *The Day After*. It could be my motto. In fact, I want a T-shirt with those words, Beneficial Irrationality, emblazoned across the front—preferably from sort of national conference of the American Economic Society. A tote bag would be nice.

When I asked if *The Day After* might have had any effect on his political activity, Nathan talked of his time studying at the Max Planck Institute, touring Europe with the Halliburtons, and registering voters. A tour for the Halliburtons was obviously a bit different from your stereotypical parade of rock and roll self-indulgence and excess.

He said, "I was doing a kind of democratic dialogue via rock shows that involved distributing voter registration cards and such."

Voter registration drives? Democratic dialogue? In Germany? Are you kidding me? Nathan was so politically active, so passionate about this stuff, that he was registering voters in *Germany*. His reach extended across oceans. He was multinational in his activism. His motto seemed to be "Think globally. Act globally." He told me that his experience with *The Day After*—along with some things Norman Mailer said—convinced him that art needs to be about engagement and activism and not about escaping reality.

This is what I was hoping to hear, but it still troubled me a bit.

Nathan made me feel inadequate in more ways than one. Aside from his artistic virtuosity and obvious intellectual acumen, he made me feel like a bad citizen. Obviously, he hadn't followed the path predicted for so many of us in this generation. He was not wallowing in a rut of angst and drugs, not slaving away at some dead-end job or spending his time designing violent video games or covering his body in expensive tattoos. He was not a money-hungry day trader, a thirtysomething dot-com retiree, or an extreme sports fanatic—or a sports fanatic at all. He was not crippled by apathy or cynicism. He was not crippled by television. He seemed to have shed the baggage of a generation, or at least turned it into something else.

Perhaps I'm overestimating the impact of *The Day After*, but part of me wants to believe that this movie had a lasting effect on a generation of artists, writers, and thinkers. The hopeful side of me—the part I inherited from my parents—wants to believe that it made us better people.

To grow up with the belief that death and destruction are imminent breeds a certain amount of passion for the present moment. It tends to make you appreciate the small things in life. It tends to make you love every day as if it were your last. It makes us—I want to argue, to believe, to hope—better husbands, wives, parents, writers, artists, and musicians.

At our best, we become individual engines of social and political change. At our best, we tour with Maynard Ferguson as a jazz prodigy, earn a Ph.D. in economics, teach, and tour and register voters and protest with our art. At our best, we use art to make meaning in a landscape shaped by a confusing muck of war, politics, and the loss of self. I was afraid that growing up with the apocalypse inevitably screws you up in the head and makes you a hopeless, psychologically paralyzed curmudgeon by the age of thirty.

This makes for a more sensational story. But perhaps it's not that way at all. Maybe the *real* story, the closest thing to truth in all of this, is a different animal altogether. If the apocalyptic generation spawns artists and intellectuals like Nathan Berg and the Halliburtons, perhaps they were right all along and *The Day After* was both the worst thing and the best thing that could have happened to us—a perfect example of beneficial irrationality.

Moving Picture

As I sat on his cramped loveseat in burning Los Angeles and listened to him talk, Nicholas Meyer started piecing it all together for me. He told me a story about a psychologist friend of his who specialized in terrorism and worked with the Reagan administration's Department of Defense in the early '80s. It was the fall of '83, and this friend was summoned to the Pentagon for a screening of Meyer's film prior to its network premiere.

Meyer's friend claimed that the Joint Chiefs of Staff, bigwigs in the military and executive branches—"people with a lot of fruit on their lapels," as Meyer put it—were all severely traumatized by what they witnessed in the film, ashen-faced and sullen. Reportedly, presidential advisor David Gergen had one question for this room full of powerful policymakers, all of them stricken by *The Day After*.

"What are we going to do about this movie?"

What they didn't do was come after Meyer and label him a communist or a socialist. He had been careful not to reveal his political leanings to the press and was, as he freely admitted, "the most capitalist SOB you'll ever meet."

They also didn't come after the science or technical aspects behind the film. Meyer's insider friend, knowing the director's work as he did, warned them off this track. Meyer had done his research before making this film. He was no TV hack. He was a professional.

Instead, in response the administration participated in an interview on ABC with Ted Koppel immediately following the broadcast. George Schultz, Reagan's secretary of state, blasted the movie for being unrealistic and simple liberal propaganda. As one would expect, he also touted the administration's position that the only reason to have nuclear weapons was for deterrence of threat from others.

On the same panel discussion, Carl Sagan also criticized the film, but for different reasons. He argued that it was entirely too optimistic and glossed over the harsh realities of a nuclear winter. Basically, though, he was also saying that it was unrealistic.

While many viewers will today report feeling quite traumatized by the movie, polls conducted immediately following the film suggested that it had little effect on the average American's feelings about nuclear war or government policy on arms proliferation.

Meyer didn't want to believe this. He didn't trust people when they testified that the movie hadn't changed them in one way or the other, and he ultimately refused to accept this response. He believed that the movie would have consequences beyond the present moment, and there is at least anecdotal evidence to suggest that, as Meyer predicted, the fallout from the movie was slow in coming but far-reaching.

In other words, I think Meyer was happy to hear me say that I was hung-up on the film, happy to have me sitting in his room telling him how his movie seriously messed with my head.

He was *trying* to mess with my head—and the heads of an entire generation.

Though privately distraught to hear that the short-term effects of the movie had been grossly exaggerated, he felt vindicated completely when he later learned of entries in Reagan's memoirs and journals about the profound effect the movie had on his psyche. Reagan's "depression" after seeing the film is actually quite well documented.

In his epic biography of the president, *Dutch,* author Edmund Morris discusses Reagan's cheerful confidence about winning the nuclear arms race against the Soviets and the dampening effect the movie had on his spirits.

> Even his optimism, however, quailed when he saw an advance print of *The Day After* . . . The image of Jason Robards walking through the radioactive ashes of Lawrence, Kansas, left him dazed, and he entered into his diary the first and only admission I have been able to find in his papers, that he was "greatly depressed."

I suspect Reagan saw something in the film—however melodramatic it might have been—that posed a threat not simply to his political agenda, but to his career, his identity, and perhaps his legacy, and *this* is what depressed him. Reagan wasn't a total dummy. He understood the power of film, that unique ability to blur the lines of reality just enough to make life magical, confusing, and even a bit depressing.

Meyer said, "I may not have changed the public's mind, but I changed one guy's mind," and he paused for effect. "I changed the president's mind," he said, glowing and puffing up a little in his seat.

Meyer was absolutely serious and committed to this idea. He said it with conviction, which is part of what makes his claims so convincing. He suggested that without *The Day After*, President Reagan would have never signed nonproliferation treaties in Reykjavik, Iceland, with Gorbachev in 1986, and he would never have even considered nuclear disarmament.

The crazy thing was that he might have been right.

In another interview I found, Meyer said, "The Reagan administration came in thinking about 'acceptable numbers' of nuclear casualties. When he signed the Intermediate Range Weapons Agreement with Gorbachev, I got a telegram from his administration that said, 'Don't think your movie didn't have any part of this, because it did.'"

Is it possible that the movie marked a shift in Reagan's ideas about foreign policy? Is it possible that this unconventional narrative, this essay, helped change the course of human history and begin the process that would result in the fall of the Soviet Union?

Knowing Reagan's susceptibility to the influence of film and knowing the raw power of the movie, the answer seems too clear to ignore. It is perhaps not just possible but more and more likely that Meyer's beliefs were indeed true and *The Day After* could have been, in Brandon Stoddard's words, "the most important movie we or anyone else ever made." It is at least possible that an obviously flawed, unrealistic movie is also a movie that was affecting enough to have helped tilt us away from the brink of nuclear conflict.

I wish I'd known as a kid that Reagan was so moved by *The Day After*. It might have made me feel a little more secure, slightly less afraid and closer to him. It seemed the days of loving and trusting your president had died with Kennedy. I was left trying to relate to our president's love for jelly beans or appreciate him because he seemed friendly with a monkey. It was tough.

Depressed or not, two weeks after the movie aired, Reagan deployed Pershing II nuclear missiles to Western Europe, ramping up the nuclear chess match to a fever pitch. Relatively few people in America batted an eye. The orgy of destruction showcased in *The Day After* didn't slow down the arms race. If anything, it seemed to speed it up and heighten enthusiasm for Reagan's policies.

Between the filming of *The Day After* and its broadcast one year later, Reagan increased his tough-guy nuclear bluster with his "Evil Empire" speech to a national evangelical Christian organization on March 8, 1983, characterizing the Soviet Union and its brand of communism as being responsible for pretty much everything bad that has ever happened in the world.

That was also the year that *Return of the Jedi*, the third (or sixth) film in the *Star Wars* series featuring the rise of the plucky, freedom-loving, and individualistic Rebel Alliance to defeat the Nazi-esque totalitarian Evil Empire in an epic space battle—sort of like *Red Dawn* in outer space. Combined with his announcement of the Strategic Defense Initiative, nicknamed the "Star Wars Defense," Reagan's foreign and domestic political rhetoric also sounded a lot like television and the movies.

WHEN HYPE IS repeated and codified, it becomes something like legend and myth. What happens when 100 million Americans (at least) remember a television experience? It gathers the collective weight of memory like a magnet. It becomes bigger than itself, larger than life. It lives forever.

Meyer also told me of a story he heard about a Cuban general who claimed that the 1962 Cuban Missile Crisis didn't seem *real*—only like just another Cold War game—until he saw a screening of *The Day After*.

I shared the stories I'd read about how the American press had trouble understanding the threat of Three Mile Island until the scientists and spokesmen began referring to the movie *The China Syndrome* in their press conferences. Suddenly the danger, the unthinkable, became thinkable. Thanks to a movie, a fiction, reality made sense. The danger was actualized and immortalized, crystallized in images. This is why Danny Dahlberg and the other characters from *The Day After* leap off the screen and speak to me in an expanded sort of hyper-reality that exists in the margins.

Meyer wondered out loud if President Harry S. Truman—who

grew up not far from Lawrence, in Independence, Missouri—might have made a different choice had he been able to see a realistic fiction about life immediately following the dropping of the bombs on Hiroshima and Nagasaki. Perhaps if there had been a cultural media experience like *The Day After* then, we wouldn't be where we are now.

THE MISSION AND message of ABC's *The Day After,* Meyer claimed, were to bring the reality of nuclear war to the forefront of the American consciousness. He wanted to galvanize belief, to temper it with fire. He wanted to punch us in the gut.

As Meyer put it to me, "I mean, what does any one of us truly believe—until we have a gun pointed at our head?", and this is when he leaned forward, made the gun shape with his hand and pointed it at me. Not at my head. More at the heart part of my body, the meaty middle of it all.

In essence, he didn't want to make a movie, he wanted to make a gun and point it at the collective consciousness of America, and he aimed right for that meaty Kansas middle and asked us, "What do you believe?" or "What do you believe when you are most afraid of death?"

Meyer wanted us to be tested, prodded, provoked, perhaps even wounded into considering our beliefs about the morality of nuclear weapons and of our president's policies. He wanted to shake us out of apathy.

Meyer has been surprisingly consistent in his thoughts on the film. I've found numerous quotes from local and national publications in '82 and '83 in which Meyer admitted to trying to make a "giant public service announcement." He never intended the film to be artful—or at least not artful in the way that narrative films are traditionally considered artful.

He wanted the film to be a kind of essay, an attempt at argument through visual rhetoric, and the TV medium was part of this essaying. Meyer will repeat this somewhat cynical assessment of his own work—*just a giant public service announcement*—but he also credits the work with changing the world.

THE EDIFYING FRIED-EGG public service announcement, in which a narrator intones, "This is your brain on drugs," first aired in 1987. *TV Guide* has voted it one of the top 100 television "advertisements" ever made. The line became almost instantly popular and was repeated, spoofed, and parodied in countless other forms.

The PSA itself made an impact not because the anti-drug message was new, but because of the rather unsophisticated and blunt use of image, symbol, and metaphor. It was not, despite what *TV Guide* says or how the drug culture embraced it, intended as an *advertisement* for anything.

It was intended to shake people up, to smack them in the face with the harsh reality of drug use and what it does to your brain (even if it wasn't necessarily factual). It was intended as artistic rhetoric and argument, a kind of miniature visual essay. It said something not only about drugs but about its audience too. It said, "Hey stupid, in case you haven't figured it out, here's the message." It was harsh and in-your-face, and it demanded a lot of engagement from the viewer. It grabbed you with metaphor and hit you with the message.

THE DAY AFTER had the visual gut punch, the moral lesson, and the idiosyncratic logic of a PSA; and unlike its big-budget counter-move, *Red Dawn*, Meyer's film eschewed a focus on character development or acting.

"Look," Meyer told me when I tried to talk with him about some of this stuff. "We had some great actors in the film, but I didn't want the movie to be about great acting. I didn't want them to talk about the amazing job that Robards or Guttenberg did with their roles. I wanted it to be about the issue, the message."

THE MESSAGE SEEMED to be that most of us were going to die pretty soon. Blame was irrelevant. Solutions were futile. What mattered was that life after the bombs wouldn't be worth living.

I told Meyer that I appreciated his use of form to convey meaning and message. I still love how all of the news and information about the building nuclear crisis is overheard on TV sets or radios, with images of characters listening to the news.

"Or not listening," Meyer pointed out, raising his finger in triumph.

"Oh yeah, one of the best scenes had to be the Hendry family with the two kids lying on the floor watching news reports about the first nuclear strikes while the parents were upstairs . . . uh . . . having sex."

"Ah, yes," he said.

I thought for a moment that I might be able to get Meyer to talk more about his craft decisions in the movie. I wanted to understand it more as art, outside the hype, away from the politics and the message.

"You know, making art is like stuffing notes in a bottle," he said while making a motion like he was rolling up a note and stuffing it into his fist. He looked like a magician tucking a red handkerchief back into his hand. "Then you toss it into the ocean and someone picks it up and . . . *pop*," he said while sticking his finger into his mouth and pulling it out, making an audible popping sound. "And you don't know what they're going to bring to the table, how that person is going to read your work. Everyone has their own idea. I can't think about that."

Perhaps Meyer didn't want to speak for the film because *The Day After* already flaunts its symbolism. The scene with the Hendrys becomes a pretty clear indictment of parents, perhaps authority in general and even of human nature. It's pure critique. We don't even know these people as well-rounded characters in a narrative. They are symbols, fleeting images, and, as a consequence, the meaning and symbolism of their actions is foregrounded and amplified.

He may have been reluctant to talk directly with me about it, but Meyer's work reveals an affinity for artfulness, perhaps even a postmodern sensibility. His acclaimed Sherlock Holmes novel, *The Seven-Per-Cent Solution*, begins with a fictional preface where, speaking directly to the reader, Meyer establishes himself as the editor of a "lost" manuscript found by his brother-in-law in an attic, wherein Watson recounts the story of how he arranged for a meeting between the famous detective Holmes—at this point hopelessly addicted to cocaine—and the renowned psychotherapist Sigmund Freud. Throughout the novel, Meyer footnotes certain passages and speaks from his editor persona, using what is basically a nonfiction form (the footnote) and a nonfiction persona (the editor) in a work of fiction. It could be described as a postmodern retelling of Sherlock Holmes.

Meyer's movie is minimalist, spare, and intense, and the reader-viewer has to do much of the work to connect the dots and understand the motivations of the characters. It is not so much artful character-ization, subtly crafted dialogue, or fine acting that accounts for the movie's power. What makes the film powerful and paradoxically realis-tic is Meyer's editing and essaying. There is degree of artful artlessness to the way he manipulates the viewer into becoming a participant in the drama.

Pretty quickly into the movie, you feel the piling up of impressions like a subliminal train wreck—this kind of urgent collage effect—and you can't look away. Even in its slower moments, the film is chaotic and anxious, frantic and intellectually dense, still difficult to sit close to. You don't so much watch *The Day After* as you *feel* it jangling through your nerves.

Meyer's relentless layering of images—aggressive and confrontational in form and pacing—hits the viewer the hardest. The fragmented, fractured narratives and jump cuts, combined with the lack of plot-driven or even character-driven narrative, make the movie *feel* like a documentary, like a very long PSA.

Because the film's craft is not hidden but openly flaunted—particularly in the scenes of missile launches and strikes, where we see those snippets of stock footage spliced together—the viewer is reminded that the film is a construct, perhaps even a piece of rhetoric, an argument.

To me, the film is a visual essay, a piece of nonfiction that employs tropes and techniques of fiction in order to explore ideas about the apocalypse, and Meyer is our essayist, our puppeteer, making the people dance for a reason.

As our time was winding down and he was getting restless, I asked Meyer what separated *The Day After* from other apocalyptic movies like *Dr. Strangelove, On the Beach, Atomic Café,* or *Testament*—a movie with a nearly identical plot to *The Day After*, but one that eschews special effects and graphic images in favor of an emphasis on character development, focusing instead on one family's struggles in the days after the bombs drop.

Meyer seemed newly energized and sat up in his seat a bit. He told me that, in addition to his editing choices, at least some of his movie's impact was amplified by television as the medium of choice. He recognized the PR value of controversy stirred up by conservative pundits like William F. Buckley and Phyllis Schlafly, who went on national television and railed against the film as liberal propaganda.

"They went out there and told Americans not to watch it," he said with a shrug and nod of surrender. "You've got to give it to Americans. If anyone tells them not to do something . . . Well, you know they're going to say: 'Hey, you can't tell me what not to watch!'"

Meyer suggested that the difference between other feature films like *Dr. Strangelove*—already distinct because of its biting satire—or *Red Dawn* and his movie is that those other films showed in theaters, sometimes only in limited markets. They were, he argued, basically preaching to the masses, to a sympathetic audience that paid money to be there. *The Day After* was trying something different.

Though he didn't come right out and say it, Meyer clearly saw his movie as more democratic, more public and political than other post-apocalyptic or anti-nuclear films.

Meyer would, I think, agree that *The Day After* belongs in a separate category altogether, perhaps not a movie at all but a mix of rhetoric, persuasion, art, and imagery—like an essay.

I persisted with comparisons. "What about other post-apocalyptic films that are more like science fiction, featuring giant killer ants or other mutants, or the comic book stories many of my generation grew up loving? You know the films, like *Planet of the Apes*, with the ubiquitous post-apocalyptic image of the Statue of Liberty toppled in the mud or encased in snow and ice?"

"Yeah, but that's easy, right? I mean, its escapist," Meyer said. "It's not real."

When he said "real," he gave a little smile and a nod, positively leprechaun-like.

The Day After made the apocalypse real. It wouldn't let you escape.

I told him that *The Day After* to me seemed more and more relevant every day, that it felt like we were reliving the '80s all over again and dwelling in a similar culture of fear. I asked Meyer what the difference was between Bush's America and Reagan's America.

He said, "It's much, much worse now."

"You really think so?" This kind of depressed me. I hoped he was going to make a joke or something. I mean, this was what I thought too, but I didn't really want to admit it. I was a father, after all, choosing to raise children in this world.

"Oh, yeah. It's different now. We don't have the Soviet Union aiming missiles at us. They're not the enemy. Everything changed after 9/11."

"How do you feel about Dick Cheney getting up there and warning us about ticking-time-bomb scenarios? Why wouldn't they make a movie about one of those attacks, a movie like *The Day After* for today?"

"It's different and worse, because what can a viewer do now to fight the threat? How can they influence policy in a way that makes a difference? We're talking now about fighting terrorism, a psychological phenomenon. It's completely different."

Meyer told me that to make a movie like that now would be pure sensationalism and fear-mongering. He suggested that the difference now is that the audience for such a movie about the new American apocalypse is too powerless, too helpless and frightened—and, I would argue, entirely too cynical, sarcastic, and ironic. We're too familiar with the techniques of *The Day After*, too conditioned to postmodern storytelling on TV and in the movies.

The audience for *The Day After* had the chance to be informed, inspired, and empowered. Meyer's movie was perhaps one of the last true democratic media events—almost like an election, an assassination, or a real war—that the country could share. It is difficult to imagine something similar happening today, mainly because nobody would ever believe it. Audiences today already know the "reality" of terrorism as it is packaged by the media. We can't avoid it. Rather than testing or galvanizing our beliefs about the methods and morality of the War on Terror, it just numbs our nerves, cauterizes our senses, and reinforces feelings of helpless apathy. Meyer thinks we will never again be in a place where a movie like *The Day After* can make a difference, or a place where a movie can matter in the same way.

Perhaps Meyer is right, but I cling to the hope that he isn't.

Changing of the Guard

11.

IT'S FUN TO shoot a gun. There's really no point denying it. I grew up shooting guns—mostly .22 rifles and a twelve-gauge Remington shotgun, maybe the occasional pistol—and I like to think that this doesn't speak to my potential for real violence. I wasn't so crazy about killing things. Didn't have the stomach for it. But shooting was a lot of fun. A rush. A gas. Maybe a little too much fun.

A movie like *Red Dawn* played right into my fears and hopes. At the age of ten, right as my parents' marriage began to crumble and *The Day After* consumed my consciousness, I became a card-carrying member of the NRA. I loved my guns.

I took classes and, at a basement firing range on the University of Kansas campus, I completed the shooting test required for what was probably a kind of junior membership. My father was very proud. Hell, I was proud, even if I didn't really share the family fun of killing small birds and preferred instead to shoot milk jugs, soda cans, bottles, or other imagined enemies. I wasn't much of a killer, but I was a good shot. I really had no idea what kind of nut jobs ran the organization or really much of anything about its politics besides vague warnings from my father about the NRA protecting our constitutional rights.

A gun-fetish film like *Red Dawn* simply confirmed my belief that guns and male friends would be the keys to my survival after the apocalypse. For years, I nurtured deep-seated fantasies about living alone in the woods, surviving off what I could scavenge and kill with my rifle and skin with my knife. I felt sure that I could kill if it was a matter of my own survival.

It's funny the ways parenthood changes you.

WHEN OUR SON was born, we lived on the Front Range of the Rocky Mountains, surrounded by military bases, oil refineries, missile silos, defense contractors, the NORAD command center, and toxic waste sites—just fifty miles or so from the Rocky Flats facility where they made the plutonium pits for every nuclear bomb built in the United States.

Our son was born into a targeted landscape—the sort of site the government told us terrorists or North Koreans or the Chinese would be striking next. If we believed Dick Cheney, all of us were taking our lives into our own hands each time we visited the mall. At some point, my dad asked me if I wanted my guns. He had them locked away in a gun cabinet, "just in case you need them someday."

But I didn't want them. And I hoped I didn't need my guns any longer. I told myself that they could probably do more harm than good, and I was pretty sure I wasn't going to raise my son with guns—even if it might prevent him from mounting an adequate defense against invading communists. But my understanding of danger had shifted, narrowed a bit. Our town had been tormented in recent months by a serial rapist who came in through open windows and doors, and I had to admit there were moments when I wished I had my twelve-gauge shotgun hidden in a closet somewhere, a handful of shells in drawer. If I was out late, Rachel slept with a screwdriver tucked between the mattress and the box spring. I didn't blame her. As the life inside her grew, my understanding of the larger world and of danger began to shift and narrow, reducing down to our small circle of family.

The night we brought our son home from the hospital, I knew something inside me had changed forever, something about my ideas of survival and the size of the world. We lived in a tiny two-bedroom house just a block from campus, located right in the middle of the rowdiest student neighborhood. Just two days old, Malcolm slept for only a couple of hours at stretch, and it was my turn to be up with him. I checked the clock and turned on the TV. It was 3:00 a.m. I paced around the small house carrying him in the crook of my arm, bouncing and singing songs, just trying to soothe him back to sleep.

He chortled and I looked down at his red-and-purple-tinted body, all shriveled up like a tiny old man with enormous white-socked feet. His neck drooped like a wet noodle, his fists curled into tiny wrinkled balls. The blood in his veins coursed just beneath thin new skin, and a fontanel on his skull pulsed rhythmically with his heartbeat.

In those moments, I swear all my fears of apocalypse began to fall and molt into something else, something much smaller and outside myself. To hold your own child in your hands—in one of the hands you inherited from your father—is to feel the entire universe in your palm, a whole tiny world of meaning pulsing and wriggling before you. It's both humbling and exhilarating, and my fears about the end of the world mutated into fears about losing my son. The apocalypse became more personal. Hopelessness was nudged aside by dreams of his future. At times it was too much to take.

I stared down at him and paced the house that night, dimly aware of the new shape of the world. The theme song for *Northern Exposure,* one of my favorite shows, had just started when I heard a racket at the side door—the sound I knew instinctively as someone turning the knob, pushing against the deadbolt lock, trying to get inside our house. It was the sound of an intruder.

I felt this instant click of resolve in my gut, this whir and hum of images, impressions, colors, and sounds. I felt suddenly—quite surprisingly—incredibly protective, almost *animal.* My hackles raised, I peeked around the corner, not sure what to expect, my senses tingling, ready for anything. It was a good thing I didn't have a gun.

Standing at the side door was not a burglar, intruder, or rapist, but a pudgy girl in a black-hooded sweatshirt—maybe seventeen or eighteen years old, and quite obviously drunk. I saw her through the glass. She teetered on the porch, methodically turning the knob. I watched her for a few moments, glad the door was locked up tight. She kept turning the knob and pushing her shoulder against the door.

I stepped up and rapped on the glass. The girl didn't move, didn't even look up at me. I knocked again, and she finally locked her wandering gaze onto me. I pointed at Malcolm curled up in my arm, his tiny red fists clutched up to his chin.

"Wrong house," I said through the glass.

She just stared, squinted her eyes, and then looked down at Malcolm. "Wrong house!" I barked.

She threw her hands up in a show of surrender, turned slowly, and fell flat on her face in our flowerbed.

I called the police, laid Malcolm down in bed next to Rachel, and watched the girl through the door until the cops arrived. She lay there in the dirt for a while, then rolled out into the driveway, sat up, and pulled the hood of her sweatshirt down over her eyes. She sat like that until the police showed, their red and blue lights pulsing and dancing across the walls of our living room. I cracked the door and gave them a statement. After trying in vain to question the drunken girl, they loaded her into an ambulance and took her to detox.

After the police left I paced around the house for a while, watching snippets of *Northern Exposure*, but I was easily distracted. I couldn't help but think about how the situation might have been different. What if I'd forgotten to lock the door? What if she made it into the house? What if she'd been a man? What if she'd hurt herself? What if I had a gun?

What worried me—frightened me, actually—was how quickly, coolly, and rationally I had decided that I could destroy anyone or anything that threatened my son. I could do bad things in the name of good, or at least in the name of my son. It was a realization both of my own capabilities but also—strangely—an expression of profound hope for the future.

My son was just two days old. I was just barely a father, still green, a man who was raised to believe that we should all be dead by now, a man trained to believe the worst. But some kind of untapped new survival instinct clicked inside and I understood perfectly, as soon as I heard that doorknob rattling, that I would do almost anything to protect him, that I could possibly kill if it was a matter of *his* survival and harm anyone who threatened his future—a future that I must have believed could be sparkling and sublime and full of possibility, a future I must have believed could be better than any I imagined.

12

DAHLBERG VARIATION: Letter to the Author

Dear Steve,

I haven't heard from you in a while . . . I understand. It's over, you know? You have to let this movie go. You have to stop dwelling . . . and ignoring Iran. North Korea. Goddamn tornados in Brooklyn. Katrina. Greensburg . . . I know you think we should meet, talk, have a cup of coffee on the surface or something. Right? You think I can provide the sort of closure you think you need, that there will be some moment between us that answers all of your questions. But the lines don't reach, don't connect . . . I can't take the risk of exposure, can't come out now. I have to stay down beneath the surface, communicating only through intermediaries, agents, editors . . . She left me, you know. Gone. Another one. Victoria. She couldn't take it any longer. I tried, Steve. I tried. Really, I did. Fuck I tried to leave. Spent just one day on the surface, lurking around the shack. Peeking out the windows like some kind of freak, some leper. A social leper. That's what I . . . No, it's not like that. It's a turtle. An ostrich. Head in the sand. That's me. An agoraphobe. That's what Victoria said. She said I had too much fear of the future and I said, "Yes! Exactly!", because I thought, stupidly, stupidly, that she understood what you and I know, Steve, what we've always known. The end is as inevitable as our preoccupation with it . . . Jesus, you should have seen the way she just threw the door open and stepped out on the porch. "Beautiful night," she said, and the wind was blowing through her hair, catching the blond strands and flinging them across her face, and the way her dress rippled and pressed over her belly . . . You should have seen it. She was trying to get me out of my own head, trying to pull me loose, jog something. But I couldn't get past the doorjamb, couldn't leave my safe territory, my bunker below the surface. I went back down, deep down. And here I can breathe again. Even though she's not up there any longer. I don't have her words, her voice whispering over the intercom, "Daaaannnny. Danny boy." That's how she woke me up in the morning. Her voice was the rising sun. Her voice was my rooster . . . And now she's gone, returned to Kansas or wherever, back to her crowd, to people her own age, other bright and sparkling cynics, the glowing ironic ones who have the luxury of psychic distance, the curse or blessing of seeing the world in shades of gray, the salve of too much stimulus, too much information . . . How much easier it is to tune out when tuning in means so little. Did this start with us? Did this begin with our generation, the wounded and bandaged ones, the kids blinded by the blast, the cathode rush, the tarnished time of Reagan and the twilight of the Cold War . . . Where will it end? Where will the ripples stop? Is there another shore in this ocean, a coast where all this shit washes up finally? I understand you have children. I know you tried to hide this from me . . . maybe because you were afraid of what I might say, afraid of the acid in my voice, my words, afraid of my scars, my eyes . . . I know that you have been using me, manipulating me, pushing me outside the frame . . . probably because you are afraid . . . because you fear your indifference, your ignorance . . . because I know you aren't telling your son everything about the new American apocalypse, because you don't really understand the legacy of this movie, because it doesn't make sense, no matter how much you write about it, you can't explain why it lingers around and you will try anything to excavate something of meaning from this text . . . But see. I'm here to tell you that there isn't much more, not much else you can find. It's mostly a story we've heard before, a story of the apocalypse, a story of divorce and the end of worlds, a story of parents doing their best to help their children survive . . . and I can't leave it behind, can't get out of the text. You're lucky, my friend. Lucky. I don't really live in the absence of fallout, can't exist beyond the screen or the page. But you will always just be sitting in the audience watching the show, waiting for the end.

    Peas.

Danny

BOOK **4**
THE RETURNING END

The Returning End

My Aunt Judy's house, June 16, 2007

There is a lot of destruction. Fortunately, a lot of folks had basements here in this part of the world and lived to see another day. Unfortunately, too many died. . . . While there was a dark day in the past, there's brighter days ahead.

—President George W. Bush's comments
upon touring Greensburg on May 9, 2007

They All Come Back

IN 1969, DURING the Summer of Love, Dad finished law school in Lawrence, and it was assumed and expected that he'd take the bar exam, pass the test, and return home to Greensburg, where he would claim his rightful place in his father's law practice handling estates and water rights issues.

That never happened.

One year later and Mom was teaching junior high school during the Days of Rage. Dad worked for the largest real estate firm in town, and I was just a heartbeat, a kick and flutter; we were already carving an orbit that would never again intersect with the family home in the way that was assumed or expected.

Once after college—some twenty-five years later—when I put my Phi Beta Kappa philosophy degree to use by painting houses for a living in Lawrence, waiting for Rachel to graduate, I showed up for one of my jobs and ran into a longtime friend of my parents. He was an old neighbor from the house in Alvamar, a nice man we knew before things went to shit for us. He asked how I was doing, and I stood there in my paint-spattered pants and told him of my plans to travel to Costa Rica and then settle, for no good reason, in Flagstaff, Arizona.

He smiled, put his hand on my shoulder, and said, "You'll come back. They all do."

I shivered, recoiled, and stammered something in response. It felt like a cult leader advising me against leaving the flock. But really, he was just voicing the expectation that many people have about Lawrence: It is a place of refuge, a place to run away from the coming storm. It's a nice place. A good place. And the assumption is always that, like Dorothy, anyone who leaves Kansas wants to come home again.

For many of us, it's just not that simple.

I DECIDED TO come home again to visit Lawrence and Greensburg in 2007, six weeks after the May 4 F5 tornado. It was Father's Day weekend. My wife was pregnant with our second child and watching her aunt fight and fade from aggressive cancer.

This was one of the first times I'd been back to Kansas in a while. I hadn't lived there for over a dozen years, and though it was hard for me to admit sometimes and even harder for my family to accept, I didn't have a strong desire to return home—mainly because home had never left me.

The Kansas I know is like a long novel I finished years ago, a novel of which I remember every word. It was a great story, filled with wonderful characters and compelling plotlines, but it was epic and psychologically cumbersome and, in many ways, mostly fiction.

The truth was that I came home to be with my dad because I wanted to spend time with him, because I thought I should help my aunt pick through the mess of her house in Greensburg, but also because I thought the trip might help me understand something more about the legacy of apocalypse in my life, or at least why I can't seem to get *The Day After* out of my head, why I can't leave the long novel of Kansas behind. I came home to find a new story.

I knew ahead of time that most of Greensburg had been rendered into piles of rubble, including the small office behind the bank where my grandfather practiced law for nearly seventy years, as well as the home where my father and his two sisters were raised, the same house where my grandparents always lived, the ice cream parlor downtown where a man named "Shakey" used to make us fountain drinks. All of it gone, crumbled, as if a bulldozer had run amok through the town for weeks.

Elsewhere the tornado raised roofs, lifted houses up and dropped them back down a few feet away, and then it just obliterated others, scouring them down to their foundations or concrete pads. Dad drove me around and showed me some of the homes he had built when he worked for a local carpenter in high school, most of them still standing at least, with the one exception being the carpenter's own house. A mobile home park on the south side of town was blown into pieces and, everywhere you looked, aluminum siding wrapped around tree trucks like hard bedsheets. Smaller chunks were sunk deep into the wood like blades.

My aunt waited out the storm in her basement, emerging in the dark to find chaos and confused, dazed citizens wandering the streets. Everything gone. People screaming and crying. The storm was the kind of tempest that made the term "apocalyptic" sound like an understatement, or just a metaphor. Words like that didn't mean much when she saw what she saw. My aunt, a very religious person, must have wondered if the rapture had come—but then surely she knew that if it had, she would have been taken. She wouldn't have been left behind. Not like this. Not like the stories say.

Whereas a category-five hurricane has sustained winds of 150 miles per hour, a wind-speed indicator in Greensburg measured 260 mph and then stopped working. Some estimates suggest the tornado hit town with wind speeds approaching 280 mph.

Eleven people lost their lives in Greensburg that night, but seeing the aftermath, even just in pictures, makes it difficult to believe anyone survived.

DAHLBERG VARIATION

Danny, won't you tell me how the radios vibrated that night with the dial-tone hum of warning. I imagine you there too, in the basement, and I wonder what you might have heard. Perhaps the TV too, its signal coming in at a slightly higher pitch, noise warbling between devices, coupled with the splash of Doppler green, orange, and red covering your town, maybe the whole corner of the state. The noise is an abomination, no help at all. So you switch it off.

Earlier, just before dusk, perhaps you sat on the sunporch with my Aunt Judy, the newly wallpapered porch, and you listened as she described how the grove of trees bent and twisted in the wind. As a beginning image, I like to put you there, the last afternoon light brushing your cheeks. One last moment of quiet in this house. You with your bandages, your scars, keeping her company in these moments.

Tell me how the noise continues. Make me hear the yellow warning sirens crank up and wail around their poles. Guide us into this space. Show me how my aunt stands at the small kitchen window above the sink and watches as the sky turns green and then bruise-colored purple. With a little help, we can see the clouds stampede, rolling and tumbling, their tendrils reaching. They are just barely discernable in these penumbral hours of the day just before the dark. Perhaps you smell the air tinged with ozone. The crackle of static. And the man on the radio tells you both it is coming—not the train that blew past on the tracks, not the morning, not salvation, not friends from church who come over sometimes in the evenings. Not yet. Not tonight. Now it is something much worse.

The man on the radio says ten minutes. You have ten minutes to take cover. But you've heard these warnings before. Ten minutes to the apocalypse. Twenty days to the end of the world. The riders are approaching.

Just a minute ago, you stood out in the front yard, staring up at the sky with your neighbors, just like you always do when it really starts to churn. You could feel the wind on your face, tugging at your cheeks, loosening the bandages over your eyes, pressing the fabric of your shirt flat against your chest.

Now you are standing in the front hall of the house, the weight of your body settled into your feet. Shoes off, toes wiggling on the rug. Waiting. Hearing. The house haunted with the ghosts of all of us. The silent piano. My brother and I peer out from walls. All the cousins. The siblings. The babies. Family Christmases. The dinner with no utensils. My grandparents. Uncle Bill sitting on a saddle mounted on a piano bench singing "I've Been So Lonely in My Saddle Since My Horse Died" and playing a tiny toy guitar. He's gone now. The children have moved away. Even I am gone, far away in California. Everyone gone from this place, this house, this town, this state. But like mortar dust blown from the joints and seams, motes of us are captured in the waning light, drifting through stray yellow beams, still lingering before your eyes, in the empty spaces between.

Fly Away Home

WHEN WE USED to return home to Greensburg as a family, everyone in town called my dad—still calls him—Eddie Church. I always chuckled a bit when I heard it. Such a diminutive name for such a big man—and not just physically big to me, but also sort of existentially big.

Dad's no "Eddie." And he doesn't like it when people call him that. I don't blame him. The name doesn't fit, and it's hard for me to imagine him fitting back into his life in Greensburg and living out the Days of Rage there instead of Lawrence. I could have been conceived in Greensburg.

Though he never practiced as an attorney, Dad's specialty in law school was in water law—a particularly relevant discipline for southwest Kansas, and one that would've suited him well working for my grandfather, who specialized in estate law. Greensburg was supposed to be where he built a life, raised a family. I could have easily been born and raised in Greensburg with my cousins. Maybe my parents would have named me Eddie Jr., and I could have worn my dad's number at the local high school, where I too would play trombone in the marching band at the halftime of my own football games.

Instead, after moving to Lawrence, Dad's own business in real estate sales, development, and property management began to take off and expand; I was born and my brother, Matt, came along eighteen months later. The prospect of moving back to Greensburg grew dimmer and dimmer. It's hard for me to imagine my mother ever agreeing to live in there, but when Dad's business collapsed eight years later and we nearly went bankrupt, he and my mom again briefly considered moving to Greensburg. There was one condition.

They would need an airplane.

"So we could fly to Denver or Kansas City or just anywhere else," my mom said by way of explanation.

"So you could escape?" I asked.

"Yes, I suppose so."

When I asked my dad to confirm this story, I expected him to contradict it in some way, or to say that it was my mom alone who demanded the airplane. I expected him to stick up for Greensburg in some way and say that he never planned to leave, that he always knew he'd come back home.

Instead he said, "Oh yeah, that was part of the deal. Had to have an airplane."

"But who would fly it?"

"I don't know," he said. "I guess me or your mom. We hadn't really got that far."

GREENSBURG WAS THE closest thing to an ancestral home I ever knew, a place from which most of my dad's family seemed to radiate out from, but it was always a strange place to me, a place that felt languid and quiet, a time capsule image of small-town life—the kind of place the writers and producers imagined Lawrence to be when they set and filmed *The Day After*.

When people find out I'm from Kansas, some of them see me in a place like Greensburg—the picture of innocence, the small-town *Wizard of Oz* image of black-and-white simplicity, and sometimes when Dad tells me his stories of pet raccoons and caves in the backyard, I think the dream is real. If I meet people from other places in Kansas and I tell them I'm from Lawrence, they will sometimes suggest that Lawrence isn't "real" Kansas. It's not a place like Greensburg. This is true. But if Kansas is more metaphor, more a state of mind or consciousness, then in some ways we're all from a place like Greensburg.

DAHLBERG VARIATION

You must have retreated to the basement by now, locked the door at the top of the stairs. Now you have the television on, the news anchors talking. Telling you things. Voices rising above the din. F5, they say. A massive beast of a tornado, they say. Over a mile wide, they say. And you think that this cannot be right, that this is too big. An exaggeration, an aberration. But it is dark outside and you see nothing beyond the white gauze, the wet panes. Now you stand in the shag-carpeted TV room, down beneath the wind, and you wait for it—suspended in the middle of this moment . . . If only we could stay there, linger for a while. But now you know that it is real, the sirens wailing on their poles for a reason. This season. This time. It's when the sirens stop, their noise winding down, dying in a slow moan, that we know you're in trouble—the proverbial calm before. The power cuts out. Lights gone. Now you cannot sit still, cannot stop pacing, rocking in the green chair, drumming your fingers on your knee and then knitting them together, tugging on your thumb. Now you are talking to God. Now you are praying, down on your knees praying with my Aunt Judy. Because you can feel the wind and the rain and the dust pushing against the foundations here, and you know that the end is coming.

Signs

THE FIRST THING Dad and I saw when we rolled into Greensburg was a big red-and-white-striped big-top circus tent on the eastern edge of town. It seemed like some kind of joke. But we stopped because it looked like the place we should be stopping to check in and get our ID badges. Nobody was allowed in without an ID badge.

But it was *not* where we were supposed to get or ID badges. A woman whose own badge identified her as a volunteer coordinator pointed us down the road, behind the Kiowa County Courthouse—one of the only buildings left standing. "Look for the portable trailers that say City Hall," she told us. Before we climbed back in the jeep, I stopped for a moment and looked around. It took a while for my eyes to adjust to the sight.

Across Highway 54 from the red-and-white circus tent were a pile of cinder blocks and wood, the remains of the Kansan Inn restaurant, baked in the sun. I tried to capture the image on a digital camera, but I quickly saw the folly of this. One frame told nothing of the story here. One fragment only part of a larger, jumbled-up jigsaw picture of this place I used to know. All of it gone now.

THAT PLACE. I pointed with the camera across the highway. Frame. Miss. That place was where I used to eat biscuits and gravy on Saturday mornings with my grandfather. That place. Point. He ate there every single Saturday. Never missed. That place was part of his routine, his ritual. I waved, not to say goodbye, but as if to wipe away the image of the shattered sign, the empty red vinyl booths caked in mud. *I've sat in those booths,* I thought. That place was where Granddad knew all the waitresses and never had to order from a menu. They just brought him a huge plate of biscuits swimming in sausage gravy. A fried egg on top. That place, that pile of concrete, where they brought me the same food, where my grandfather looked on admiringly as I ate the huge pile of sausage and flour and grease. That place. Right now, that place was a pile of stone and wood, a revision of my memories. That rubble was nothing I recognized, just a pile. And I didn't know what to do with it, how to make sense of it.

So we climbed back in the jeep and drove down 54, into the heart of the destruction, passing Dillon's grocery store—the only one in town—where my grandmother used to let me pick anything I wanted, filling our cart with Pepsi and Nutter Butter cookies, ice cream and half-and-half milk for our cereal in the mornings. Most of the building was gone, peeled away and tossed. The only grocery store now was forty miles away in Pratt, the biggest city around at 20,000 residents.

The Kiowa County Courthouse, a building I'd barely noticed before but one in which my granddad spent countless hours, now loomed over everything. With a large brick-and-stone edifice, it had been damaged, battered on the south side, but it still stood above everything else. The high school next door was already being bulldozed down and loaded into dump trucks.

All around the courthouse, white trailers were packed in, blocking streets and filling up empty spaces. A small city of full-size single-wide mobile home trailers and several rows of tiny duplex FEMA trailers occupied what used to be rarely filled parking lots.

It took some time for us to find the City Hall trailer and, when we did, it was closed. But we did find a FEMA office which was, as it turned out, the place to go to get the ID badges.

My ID badge identified me as a Greensburg resident, and I felt horribly sheepish and guilty for wearing it. Despite my role as outsider, interloper, and parasite, despite feeling like a disaster tourist, I share a name with my grandfather, a town lawyer, a man who presided over the school board, the Rotary Club, the Masons, and the chamber of commerce, a man responsible for raising the money to build the Methodist Church and instrumental in the development of the Big Well as a tourist destination and defining feature of Greensburg—a legitimate pillar of the community.

I was afraid that people would stop me, stare at the name, stare at me, and shake their heads. "Nope," they'd say. "I knew Steve Church, and you're not him."

SOME DAYS I wanted to believe that Greensburg was the kind of place where we could live, a place where they wouldn't think about building a nuclear power plant and where there was still a drug store downtown with a soda fountain, a place far removed from the dangers of the larger world—but the truth is that I couldn't imagine living in Greensburg, couldn't imagine raising a family in this tiny shell without wanting to dig my way out or hop an airplane to anywhere else. When I saw myself there, I saw myself sitting alone in a darkened room with a beer in one hand, only the glow of the television illuminating my face.

THE ID BADGE listed my address as my Aunt Judy's house. This was, of course, a lie. I never lived in my Aunt Judy's house—at least not in the way you live in most places. I lived there in the stories, the images that surface in odd moments: wheeling around the basement in my cousin Aaron's yellow wheelchair, my uncle Bill sitting on a saddle on the piano bench dressed in cowboy garb and wearing a too-small straw hat as he strummed a toy guitar and sang "I've Been So Lonely on My Saddle Since My Horse Died," and that Christmas dinner, or maybe Thanksgiving, when we ate the entire meal without silverware, just fingers, carrot sticks, and celery stalks for scooping and spooning. I never lived in her house but it lived in me, as did my grandparents' home near the elementary school, the house where my father was raised.

The picture on my ID badge captures most of my torso and was taken at an odd angle, my right shoulder cut off. There is a white backdrop but my head rises over it, the top line of it bisecting my head at the top of my ears. I don't look happy or sad. Just sort of tired, and when I look at it now I'm reminded of my confusion at the time. *Do I smile for my FEMA badge picture?*

That didn't seem quite right. But I didn't want to look dour or sad-faced, because that would be against the general gestalt of Western Kansas people. Even after the end of their world, everything was looking up. Everyone was positive. Suffering was done silently, privately, stoically. Work took the place of public grief. Nobody complained in Greensburg.

Dad and I exited the trailer into the bright sun. I stepped onto a sidewalk and looked down. Words. Written on the pavement. Maybe with a permanent marker. Maybe paint.

We survived F5! Trevor, May 5, 2007.

This was not the only sign we would see. Everywhere, it seemed, people had marked up the rubble and wrecks with spray paint and other instruments. I saw the odd rune-like scratchings of rescuers, warnings to looters and reporters, praise for Jesus, and, beneath the corner of one dislodged house, fake legs dressed in red-striped stockings and black pointy shoes, and the words *There's no place like home* spray-painted on the siding.

THE ONLY RECOGNIZABLE sign of my dad's childhood house was the basement. The house had been sold a few years before, after my grandparents both died within a year of each other of complications related to Alzheimer's and cancer. Now it was just gone. Wood and brick and dirt filled my grandmother's sewing room, but the yellow-and-black Fallout Shelter sign still hung over the door. One wall had caved in and covered the floor with mud.

From what little was left, I could just barely discern the outlines of the mollusk-like old house, the added-on rooms, and the garage. It's a house where I spent countless Christmas mornings and long days in the hot summers, where I'd marveled at the extra-thick spongy carpet in the living room, the glass shelves filled with porcelain figurines, and my grandmother's electric organ. Now it looked so small, so insubstantial. The basement, where my grandfather kept his old typewriters, had seemed cavernous and mysterious to me—now it looked tiny, bare, and sad.

"Was this the spot?" I asked, standing on a patch of mud in the corner of the yard. The hedge was long gone. I wanted to know where the cave had been.

"Yep, that's it," Dad said, and I asked him to help me visualize the size of his backyard cave, the place where the tunnel came out, all those details so I could try to remember it later. But it was too much to remember, too hard to capture everything. I'd never seen anything like this kind of destruction.

Everywhere we looked, it seemed, were hundreds of stuffed animals—their pink-and-yellow fur matted with dirt, their cotton bodies waterlogged and bloated. We saw toy animals and doll babies, those cherubic Cabbage Patch Kids and the brightly colored plastic of children's toys all tossed together with wood, mud, brick, and mortar.

The trees around my grandparents' house—everywhere in town—were gone or ripped down, attenuated stumps, the limbs torn off, the bark peeled back. My father's hole in the ground was perhaps just a distant dream, the ghost of a memory, a relic of the lost world.

We climbed back into the Jeep and headed for my Aunt Judy's. Outside the hospital, the staff had lined the beds up like soldiers in the parking lot, and someone wedged an American flag into one of them. It hung limp and rippled slightly in the breeze as we passed.

MY AUNT JUDY'S house was one of the largest houses in Greensburg. It had a stately brick drive, old iron gates, massive cedar trees like sentinels against the wind, a grove of cherry trees, and original stained glass in the doors and windows. The train tracks ran right along the northern edge of the property, but I swear I never noticed the noise and rumble, the piercing horn of the freight trains—probably because the trees insulated the house from the sound.

It was a beautiful home—one that had, for many years, occupied a space in my brain reserved for images of ideal homes, the kinds of places in which epic nineteenth-century narrative novels are centered. The entire house had been trimmed out in thick walnut and oak, and it seemed labyrinthine to a child thanks to two different basement staircases, a top-floor "ballroom" that ran the length and width of the house, and closets always filled with toys and costumes.

When Dad and I came upon the old house that day, the top floor was gone, the grand front porch was partially collapsed, and several cracks snaked up the front, making the house seem to tilt to the north, away from the blast of the storm. It looked to me as if it was just moments away from collapsing completely. It was hard to imagine how Aunt Judy could have survived.

The ground floor of the house was filled with the mulch of interior furnishings, glass, wood, and porcelain. The carpet and walls were waterlogged and spattered with mud. I entered through the boarded-up door, beneath the partially collapsed porch, and found the joists soaked and arched up through the carpet like the ribs of some buried beast. The windows were all gone, the furniture tossed around, everything reeking of mildew and mold. After the tornado passed, it rained for days on the High Plains, filling the battered houses with water, soaking furniture, clothes, everything.

I found the upstairs a confusing jumble of furniture, plaster, mattresses, doors, brick, and lumber. I couldn't even recognize it as a place I knew. We climbed over a pile of brick and up a staircase to the top level, to a small platform of wood flooring still left that let us look down into the rooms below and out across the shattered and broken landscape of life after an apocalypse. Standing in that spot, taking it all in, there was no question that a world had ended.

6

DAHLBERG VARIATION

Now. This is it . . . wish . . . for something different. Not the ting. Creak. Roar when it hits. Smacks the house like a backhand slap, a wave that never breaks. And the pop-pop-pop like fireworks. Like gunshots. You have to stop thinking what it means and how it sounds. You have to just listen. Blink, shake the dust out of your hair. Both of you. Wish, wish you knew who in the roar . . . who to call to reach above the noise. Noise not like a train. Like a train wreck in the dark. Glass breaking. Now how the wind howls. Now the house is groaning. And you are curled up with your head tucked between your knees, your hands clasped behind your head like we learned in school. You are waiting. Spinning. Drifting off. The furniture scrapes on the floors upstairs, slams into the walls. The piano's cabinet resonates blows from flying debris. Certainly parts of the house are gone now. Certainly things will never be the same. The house shudders and shakes. Now you understand. Now you begin to think too that God has done this. Now you want to tell yourself that this is all part of his plan. The plan. The grand plan. Because it is easier to believe that this sort of random violence happens for a reason, a purpose, a punishment. But there is no reason in weather. No rhyme, no order, no morality in the storm. You are in no position now to appreciate the false prophecy of the TV meteorologist, because right now you long for his baritone voice, his reassuring confidence, his perfectly coiffed hair. You want him to be the one to say, "It's over. It's all over." Any voice besides the howl of the storm. Perhaps my voice? What if? What if I had decided to call you, or my aunt, out of the blue? Something I rarely do, if ever. There are no lines of communication between us. What if we had been on the phone and I had heard the sirens wailing in the background, the pinched fear in her voice? What if things were different? What if she could travel too, like you, all the way to California? Perhaps I could have come home then, carried by the winged monkeys.

It is almost over now . . . and there is profound quiet in the sudden absence of violence. Much greater than the calm before is the calm after, the come-down, the drop. The drain. This is when you wait in the dark for some sign. Anything. A light, a voice. The crackle of static and the radio's words. The whisper of the leaving wind as it races out beyond your house on the edge of town, rises up, scatters, and dissipates, dropping cars and scraps in the reservoir, wrapping the trees with shirts and sheet metal. The funnel loses fuel, sucks back up. Disappears. Gone.

You are still down below, in the basement with the plastic toy oven and the dress-up clothes, the antique trucks and rag dolls. But you will find your way up. And you will rise from the basement into the kitchen, holding each other's hands for balance. In the half-light it seems like the kitchen we knew before, everything mostly intact. It's only when our eyes adjust to the dark and you stumble out into the dining room, tilt your ear to the churning sky. Only when you climb the stairs to rooms that no longer exist. The top two floors of the giant home cleaved, torn with the roof and tossed. This is when we know. This is when we understand you have survived.

In the air, we hear the *flap-flap* of giant wings. People screaming. No sirens. The woman nearby with her legs broken. The neighbor cursing. A rustle in the rubble, the stripped limbs. The confusion of birds. And behind it all, the soft *shuffle*, *thump*, and *tap* of hand talk in the attenuated trees.

7

Deflection

After we returned from Greensburg, Dad moved out of the trailer at the asphalt plant and into an air-conditioned cubicle space at a small start-up company in Lawrence focused on nanotechnology, or the creation of tiny disease-fighting nanoparticles, invisible to anything but the most powerful microscopes, thousands of times smaller than the width of a human hair.

His new job is to design the facilities and machines required to produce these nanoparticles, which are used to fight cancer, heart disease, perhaps even things like Alzheimer's. This move, this job—it seems like a lie, a non sequitur at least. Nanotechnology? Really?

When people ask me what my dad does, I tell them, "He builds stuff. Systems. He makes things run."

Dad went from turning an asphalt plant from a money-loser into a profit-making operation, to building complicated chemical machines made to cure the incurable. Asphalt to Alzheimer's. Gravel to nanoparticles. This is what I've come to expect from Dad. He is a survivor. There's no doubt about that. Last year he had a three-by-six-inch chunk of flesh removed from his chest and a lymph node excavated from his armpit. Stage-four melanoma. Malignant. But it didn't appear to have metastasized. He didn't tell me about it until after he got the test results. No radiation necessary. No chemotherapy. But it still scared the shit out of me.

The year before that, Dad tripped on a garden hose, fell, and hit his head on a rock. He saw stars for a few seconds, but got up and shook it off. He never mentioned it, except maybe to my stepmother. It was just a bump on the head, he thought. No big deal.

For months afterward, though, Dad suffered pounding headaches, and, while he didn't recognize it at the time, he also had problems with his memory and speech. He would lose words, simple ones, and trail off mid-sentence. He'd be driving and forget where he was going.

He went to doctors and chiropractors, each of them with a different diagnosis. But because he'd never gone to the hospital when he fell and hit his head, there was no record of this injury. Finally, he was given a CAT scan.

He got the call on a weekend. *Subdural hematoma.* A big one. A blood clot about the width of a fist, thick and bullish. It had squashed the left side of his brain, taking up space in his skull. He needed brain surgery. Two days later, doctors drilled a hole in his skull and inserted a stent to relieve pressure and drain the clot. By many conservative estimates, he narrowly averted death.

THE ACCIDENT WAS such a dumb thing. Dad was just standing at his barbecue grill, enjoying an average day at the lake. He stepped away from the grill, got his foot tangled in a garden hose, and toppled over.

Dad was nearly killed in a barbecue accident.

It wasn't funny. But it was. Or I didn't know how to deal with my father's mortality, so I joked about buying him a grilling helmet or about the medal he won at the X-Games for extreme freestyle grilling. This was how we dealt with the fear. We deflected it with humor, distancing ourselves from the reality.

When he went in for brain surgery, I was scared. I was afraid for him. So I called my mom. Just like always. A thousand miles away in Phoenix, I think she was scared too—for him, for me, for herself. I could hear the worry in her voice. Though she'd been far away from him for years, she'd never left completely.

I also realized that since the divorce the only times the three of us have been in a room together for extended periods of time were for family therapy, *The Day After*, my brother's funeral, my college graduation, and my wedding, and it strikes me that it may not happen again until another one of us dies. Those factional years of the early '80s marked a divide for me, the death of one life and the dawn of another, and many days I still find myself staring into the yawning chasm.

WHEN WE STROLLED around the streets of Greensburg, Dad taking me on the sadness tour of places that used to be, I realized that my father was only then beginning to seem old, vulnerable, even fragile sometimes. It didn't seem right that he should have to worry about starting over again. It didn't seem right that his parents should die and then his hometown be completely destroyed. But he would never admit as much to me. To him and to everyone I met in Greensburg, there was no blame, no self-indulgent mourning, only a focus on the next hour, day, month, maybe year. I had never expected to feel such peace in the midst of such violent destruction.

On our tour, we stopped for lunch at the parking lot where the Methodist Church used to be and ate some sort of soggy stroganoff. But the bad food didn't matter. We were surrounded by people who knew my father, my grandparents, my aunt, my uncle, and all my cousins. I met a man who had known my grandfather for almost 70 years, and I watched my dad smile and shake hands, and nobody called him Eddie. Even if they had, he wouldn't have cared. He would have written in big black marker on a nametag Hello, My Name Is Eddie Church, and he would have been happy to call Greensburg home.

After lunch, as we drove again, out south of town to see if we could trace the path of the twister, Dad admitted that he hadn't felt so at home in Greensburg since he was a boy.

"I never understood why anyone would come back here after the storm until that lunch," he said. "That was pretty cool."

Later, as we drove and talked, he showed me where skin and hair had grown over the hole in his head, where the bone would never grow back, and I pushed the soft pad of my fingertip into the hole, learning the edges of it, feeling the tickle of his buzz-cut hair.

"So if you ever need an ice-pick lobotomy, that's the spot?" I asked.

"That's it," he said. "Just get through the skin and you go straight to brain."

He told me how he'd been doing sudoku puzzles, listening to language tapes, and forcing himself to use a computer mouse left-handed, even taking different routes to and from work—all in an effort to exercise his recovering brain. He told me he felt like a new person—smarter, sharper, quicker, and more coordinated, almost reborn in the same body. He didn't say it, but I thought, *like a mutant, a superhero or something.*

Now this. Another job. Another end. Another new beginning.

Now he will be putting that brain, those abilities to the test once again, trying to cure cancer, Alzheimer's, and diseases of the heart.

DAHLBERG VARIATION

This is how it ends. A man in a truck finds you. Wandering east along Highway 54. Away from town, back toward Lawrence. This man, a farmer. A simple man in a simple truck. He has driven to Greensburg to search for his own parents. He picks you up, perhaps because you look like his mother for a split second, perhaps because you look like a boy he knows, perhaps because he actually knows you from church. He picks you up because that's all he can do. He listened to the storm on the radio, watched the red cloud pass over the TV screen. He asks your name, but you are disoriented. Dazed. Perhaps in disbelief. He asks about your eyes and you want to tell him how the storm sounded, how it was nothing like a freight train, and you want to tell him about the piano, the pictures, the Big Well, the winged monkeys, and the wolves that will come. The bugs. The roaches released. You want to tell him about the special kind of mutant it takes to survive something like this, about the anger, the green rage, the strength to make a difference, but in the after-light of a storm-fractured moon, you can only close your eyes and listen for the flutter of wings, the lift and float of flight, and next to you in the truck, the soft thumping of my Aunt Judy's vibrant heart.

Birds

THE TORNADO TURNED the stately and aristocratic grove of cherry trees north of my aunt's house into a pile of naked limbs and amputated stumps. Around the trunks of the few remaining trees, small green tufts of leaves and branches had begun to sprout like neck plumage on a duckling.

Six weeks away from the storm and the flora had just begun to return. Tom Corns, president of the Greensburg State Bank, guessed the town would lose half of its population, leaving it with around 500 or 600 residents. People had already started buying up lots, bulldozing the remaining structures, filling in basements, and expanding their smaller lots into grand estates. The streets in town were wide and accommodating. Soon a crew of "green" builders would come from the University of Kansas in Lawrence to build an arts center and eco-friendly homes, and a crew of television cameras would record every minute of the drama.

The trick with Greensburg would be to try and lure not only residents but also retail businesses back to town. Someone had offered a warehouse full of new clothes, mostly closeouts and other stuff found in the outlets, but there was nowhere to put it all. The downtown area of Greensburg looked like what the film crew wanted Lawrence to look like for *The Day After*. It was a long pile of brick, the rubble of a dismantled city. The only similar thing I'd ever seen was a church in Dresden, Germany, that had been left as a reminder of the infamous Allied firebombing raids of February 13, 1945.

My dad told me that a Boy Scout troop from suburban Kansas City had offered the people of Greensburg two truckloads of equipment, enough to outfit a troop of seventy boys, but Tom Corns said the Boy Scout troop in town—the same one in which my Dad had been a member and an Eagle Scout—had three, maybe four active members. It seemed that I wasn't the only one who didn't know how to help.

THE DAY WAS almost over. Earlier, miraculously, my cousin had found my aunt's diamond earring in the mess and ruin of her house, but such grace had long since left the scene and nobody could find the red box she really wanted, the box with stuff that mattered—letters and personal things from her husband, mostly of sentimental value, the hardest kind of value to replace.

We would be gone soon—the visitors and voyeurs. Tomorrow a man with a bulldozer and dump truck would knock the house down, rip out the basement, and haul it all away. Tomorrow there would be nothing left here but a hole in the ground. Tomorrow my Aunt Judy would leave Greensburg and try not to look back. The only places I'd ever known here were now vacant lots, piles of rubble, or muddy holes.

The family cabin in Colorado. The house in Alvamar. Now my granparents' house and Aunt Judy's home. Slowly but surely, the places of my past, the places of my family history, seemed to be disappearing; and I realized that I would have to map my own landscapes of survival and make my own homes—wherever we might be living. I thought of my son and my wife and the new baby thumping around inside her belly back in California, and I somehow felt like my search had ended, or at least changed direction.

I stood out on what used to be my aunt's front lawn—now a chaotic jumble of mud, lumber, and tree stumps—with my dad, Aunt Judy, my cousin Cindy, and her husband, Rod, all of us lingering in waning sun.

"See that," Cindy said, pointing up at a tree.

I gazed up. High in the denuded limbs of a cedar, a scrap of tattered white fabric fluttered in the breeze.

"That's my bridal veil," she said and sort of shrugged.

It was eerily still and quiet—except for the low rumble of bulldozers and the beeping of their back-up alarms. In the distance, the faint sound of hammering and the occasional whine of a power saw. Nothing else. Weather reports had warned of another storm, another possible tornado. It never ends.

"You know," my Aunt Judy started, and then stopped.

We all looked at her.

"The day after the storm, there were huge flocks of birds wheeling around in the sky, circling and circling overhead, looking for their nests, I suppose. The next day they were all gone."

Statue outside my Aunt Judy's house, June 16, 2007

Baby's tombstone in Greensburg cemetery.
Reads: *Born JUL26, 1925. Died JUL26, 1925. God Bless Our Darling Baby*

Appendix 1

Jason Robards	*Dr. Russell Oakes (father, doctor)*
Georgann Johnson	*Helen Oakes (mother)*
Kyle Aletter	*Marilyn Oakes (daughter)*
JoBeth Williams	*Nurse Nancy Bauer*
Steve Guttenberg	*Stephen Klein (as Steven Guttenberg)*
John Lithgow	*Joe Huxley*
John Cullum	*Jim Dahlberg (father, farmer)*
Doug Scott	*Danny Dahlberg (son, blinded)*
Ellen Anthony	*Joleen Dahlberg (daughter, younger)*
Bibi Besch	*Eve Dahlberg (mother)*
Lori Lethin	*Denise Dahlberg (daughter, older)*
Amy Madigan	*Alison Ransom*
William Allen Young	*Airman Billy McCoy*
Clayton Day	*Dennis Hendry*
Antonie Becker	*Ellen Hendry*
Jeff East	*Bruce Gallatin*
Madison Mason	*TV Host*
Calvin Jung	*Dr. Sam Hachiya*
Lin McCarthy	*Dr. Austin*
Dennis Lipscomb	*Reverend Walker*
Alston Ahern	*Cynthia*
William Allyn	*Professor*
Pamela Brown	*Nurse*
Jonathan Estrin	*Julian French*
Stephen Furst	*Aldo*
Arliss Howard	*Tom Cooper*
Rosanna Huffman	*Dr. Wallenberg*

Barbara Harris — *Cleo Mackey (as Barbara Iley)*
Bob Meister — *Cody*
Vahan Moosekian — *Mack*
George Petrie — *Dr. Landowska*
Glenn Robards — *Barber #2*
Tom Spratley — *Barber #1*
Stan Wilson — *Vinnie Conrad*

Abbreviated Film and TV Diaspora from www.imdb.com

Nicholas Meyer

1984	*Star Trek II: The Wrath of Khan*, film, writer, director
1988	*The Deceivers*, film, director
1986	*Star Trek IV: The Voyage Home*, film, writer
1991	*Star Trek VI: The Undiscovered Country*, film, writer
1997	*The Odyssey*, film for TV, executive producer
1998	*The Prince of Egypt*, film, writer
1999	*Vendetta*, film for TV, director
2003	*The Human Stain*, writer
2008	*Elegy*, film, writer
2009	*Don Quixote*, film, director

Edward Hume

1985	*John and Yoko: A Love Story*, film for TV, writer
1988	*Stranger on My Land*, film for TV, writer
1990	*Common Ground*, film for TV, writer
1992	*Deceptions*, film, writer
1997	*Flood: A River's Rampage*, film for TV, writer

Jason Robards / Dr. Russell Oakes (father, doctor)

1984	*You Can't Take It with You*, film for TV, Grandpa Martin Vanderhof
1984	*Sakharov*, film for TV, Andrei Sakharov
1985	*The Long Hot Summer*, film for TV, Will Varner
1988	*The Good Mother*, film, Muth
1989	*Reunion*, film, Henry Strauss
1989	*Black Rainbow*, film, Walter Travis
1990	Nine episodes from *The Civil War*, TV, Ulysses S. Grant
1991	*The Perfect Tribute*, TV, President Abraham Lincoln

1991   *Chernobyl: The Final Warning,* film for TV, Dr. Armand Hammer
1991   *Mark Twain and Me,* film for TV, Mark Twain
1992   *Lincoln,* film for TV, President Abraham Lincoln
1994   *The Enemy Within,* film for TV, General R. Pendleton Lloyd
1998   *Enemy of the State,* film, Congressman Phillip Hammersley
1999   *Magnolia,* film, Earl Partridge

Steve Guttenberg / Stephen Klein

1984   *Police Academy,* film, Carey Mahoney
1985   *The Ferret,* film for TV, Sam Valenti
1985   *Police Academy 2: Their First Assignment,* film, Carey Mahoney
1985   *Cocoon,* film, Jack Bonner
1986   *Police Academy 3: Back in Training,* film, Sgt. Carey Mahoney
1987   *Police Academy 4: Citizens on Patrol,* film, Sgt. Carey Mahoney
1987   *3 Men and a Baby,* film, Michael Kellman
1988   *Cocoon: The Return,* film, Jack Bonner
1990   *3 Men and a Little Lady,* film, Michael Kellam
1993   "Love of Limits" from *CBS Schoolbreak Special,* TV, Tom Hardgrove
1997   *Casper: A Spirited Beginning,* film for TV, Tim Carson
1997   *Tower of Terror,* film for TV, Buzzy Crocker
2005   *The Poseidon Adventure,* film for TV, Richard Clarke
2005–   Eight episodes from *Veronica Mars,* TV, Woody Goodman
2006
2007   One episode of *Law & Order: Criminal Intent,* TV, Clay Darren Sr.

John Lithgow / Joe Huxley

1984   *2010,* film, Dr. Walter Curnow
1984   *The Adventures of Buckaroo Banzai Across the 8th Dimension,* film,
        Lord John Whorfin/Dr. Emilio Lizardo
1984   *Footloose,* film, Reverend Shaw Moore
1986   *The Manhattan Project,* film, John Mathewson
1987   *Harry and the Hendersons,* film, George Henderson
1991   *At Play in the Fields of the Lord,* film, Leslie Huben
1993   *The Pelican Brief,* film, Smith Keen
1995   "You, Murderer" from *Tales From the Crypt,* TV, Dr. Oscar Charles
1995   "Someone to Watch Over Me" from *Frasier,* TV, Madman Martinez
2000   *Don Quixote,* film for TV, Don Quixote de La Mancha/Alonso
        Quixano
1996–   139 episodes of *3rd Rock from the Sun,* TV, Dr. Dick Solomon
2001

2000	*Rugrats in Paris: The Movie,* film, Jean-Claude
2001	*Shrek,* film, Lord Farquaad
2004	*Kinsey,* film, Alfred Seguine Kinsey
2005	$E=mc^2$, film for TV, narrator
2005	"Einstein's Big Idea" from *Nova,* TV, narrator
2006–2008	13 episodes from *Twenty Good Years,* TV, John Mason

John Cullum / *Jim Dahlberg (father, farmer)*

1989	"Catch a Falling Star-May 21, 1979" from *Quantum Leap,* TV, John O'Malley
1990–1995	110 episodes from *Northern Exposure,* TV, Holling Vincouer
1997	*The Secret Life of Algernon,* film, Algernon Pendleton
1998	Eight episodes from *To Have & to Hold,* TV, Robert McGrail
1997–2000	Fifteen episodes of *ER,* TV, David Greene
2000	"The Convention" and "Into the Woods" from *Roswell,* TV, James Valenti Sr.
2006	*The Night Listener,* film, Pap Noone
2003–2009	Nine episodes from *Law and Order: Special Victims Unit,* TV, Judge Barry Moredock

Doug Scott / *Danny Dahlberg (son, blinded)*

With the exception of *The Day After,* Doug Scott's work in the movie industry has been primarily behind the scenes as a cameraman or set dresser. He currently works as a camera operator for the Nickelodeon series *True Jackson, VP.* But he has also worked on the following TV shows and films, *Pirates of Silicon Valley* (TV movie), *Murphy Brown* (TV series), *Dave's World* (TV series), *Room for Two* (TV series), *My Stepmother Is an Alien* (film), *The Mafu Cage* (film), *Chicken Soup for the Soul* (TV series), *Everything's Relative* (TV series)

Ellen Anthony / *Joleen Dahlberg (daughter, younger)*

Bibi Besch / *Eve Dahlberg (mother)*

| 1984–1985 | Three episodes from *Dynasty,* TV, Dr. Veronica Miller |

1985	"Mothers" from *Dallas*, TV, Dr. Gibson
1988	Two episodes from *Family Ties*, TV, Dr. Hewitt
1988	One episode from *Knots Landing*, TV, Dr. Sarah Gilbert
1989	*Steel Magnolias*, film, Belle Marmillion
1990	*Betsy's Wedding*, film, Nancy Lovell
1992–1993	"Grosse Pointe, 48230" and "Burning Down the House" from *Northern Exposure*, TV, Jane O'Connell
1994	"Revenge Is the Nuts" from *Tales from the Crypt*, TV, Armelia
1996	"Woman of the Year" from *Dr. Quinn, Medicine Woman*, TV, Beatrice Cartwright
1999	*California Myth*, film, Harriet (her last film or TV role)

Appendix 2
Notes, Acknowledgments, and Addenda

Book 1: In the Beginning

Chapter 1: Much of the story of Quantrill's raid and the quotes from Rev. Fisher in this chapter are adapted or taken from accounts of the events on the immensely helpful website www.kuhistory.com, where you can read much more about Quantrill's raid, the Days of Rage, and *The Day After*. For a contemporary vision of Quantrill, you could check out Ang Lee's 1999 yawner, *Ride with the Devil*, starring Toby Maguire. It is, perhaps, interesting to note that Ang Lee, who clearly harbored some fascination with Quantrill, also made the first big-budget CGI *Incredible Hulk* film.

The term "Jayhawker" originally referred to anti-slavery guerrilla fighters who clashed with neighboring pro-slavery guerrilla fighters from Missouri, who were in turn regularly referred to as "border ruffians" and "bushwhackers." The term Jayhawker now often applies to a student or alumnus of the University of Kansas, and to fans of the university sports teams, as well as to the mascot, the Jayhawk—a mythical raptor with a stout blue body, large red head, a nearly pelican-sized yellow beak, and big yellow boots.

Chapter 2: It is perhaps worth noting, if only to continue patterns in the book, what (at least according to various online sources) also occurred on April 20: In 1939, Adolph Hitler was born. In 1953, Project BLUEBIRD turned into Project MKULTRA. BLUEBIRD and MKULTRA were code names for alleged CIA mind-control experiments in the 1950s and '60s that involved dosing unwitting subjects, including children, with LSD. In 1978, Korean Air Lines Flight 902 was shot down by the Soviets. This was the first (but not the last) Korean Air Lines plane shot down by Soviet fighter jets. A rocket punched a hole in the fuselage and the rapid decompression killed two passengers. The left wing was also severely damaged, forcing the plane to make an emergency landing on a frozen lake in Siberia. Surprisingly, 107 passengers and crew survived. In 1979, on April 20, President

Jimmy Carter was attacked by a swamp rabbit while on vacation in Plains, Georgia. Native to the Southern United States, the swamp rabbit can weigh as much as six pounds and is a skilled swimmer. While fishing on a pond, President Carter was charged by an agitated swamp rabbit and forced to splash water at it with a paddle to fend off the attack.

Chapter 3: This chapter is adapted from a section in my first book, *The Guinness Book of Me: A Memoir of Record* (Simon & Schuster, 2005), and used in both cases to show the early influence my childhood illness had on my personality as well as my active imagination and general fearful fascination with apocalyptic scenarios.

Chapter 4: One night, very late, as I was doing research for this book, I found a washingtonpost.com discussion forum on Three Mile Island and many of the voices seemed familiar: *I was in Thule Greenland at the scene of another nuclear accident—a nuclear weapons accident that was classified until 1996 . . . When I heard that my hometown was in peril I wondered if I would ever see it again. All of a sudden the radiation signs at the Thule Air-base which were about 18 inches square seemed to be 10 feet square! . . . I hear of many people with thyroid trouble . . . I grew up in Marysville, a small town north of Harrisburg. I remember looking at my block, wondering if I was ever going to see it, or the people I lived near, again . . . Two of three days into the crisis, around 9 p.m., all the lights in town went out. We later found out that a car struck a utility pole, but no one knew it then . . . I was born in Harrisburg . . . Of course, as a child I had no idea what those big towers were. After leaving, they were a landmark that told me that we were almost to Grandma's house . . . I had one uncle who owned a grocery store across the river who stayed to take advantage (of) all the reporters and curiosity seekers in the area . . . I was a senior engineer on the nuclear engineering staff of BG&E at the time. I recall . . . a feeling of awe and humility that the technology we thought was foolproof wasn't . . . Although I wish the accident had never happened, I truly believe that it confirmed the quality of our nuclear plants and effectiveness or our defense-in-depth philosophy . . . I was a single parent of a very active three year old, who was blessed with the chicken pox during the accident . . . I was only 5 years old when the accident happened, but remember being afraid to go outside. It is one of my earliest childhood memories . . . We were living in Juniata County, PA when the disaster occurred . . . My grandmother was diagnosed with thyroid cancer and now suffers through (how ironic) radiation treatments. My mother and I have both been diagnosed with hypothyroidism . . . With Three Mile Island, we couldn't see the danger, but we knew if this "flood" hit, we could never come back . . . I can remember wearing a*

T-shirt that said "Some prayed. We stayed." And the name of the company they worked for along with the date of the accident. I have a photo of my grandfather working inside after the accident. My grandfather died at the age of 59 . . . the turning point was the announcement to evacuate pregnant women and children within a five-mile radius . . . I will never forget how sunny it was that Wednesday morning . . . what matters is the wind and if the radiation plume carrying the largest dose happened to be where you were those days. I was also struck by the fact that the Amish people in Lancaster who don't even use electricity were subject to this horror that resulted from our modern lifestyle. Ironic and sad. I'll never be the same . . . the movie paralleled the events at the TMI plant to an uncanny degree . . . Although a significant number of students also departed, many remained for a weeklong party of now unimaginable proportions. Ah, the recklessness of youth . . . I grew up within 5 miles of the power plant . . . I remember that we came back inside from a recess and the teachers seemed very nervous and kept us in our rooms. Periodically the teacher would come into the room and say, "Johnny, you [sic] mother is here" and the child would leave . . . At some point, the teachers told us about the accident and the possibility that the area would be too dangerous to live in for 40 years if the worst happened. The world seemed a very chaotic, scary thing to a small group of 5th graders that day.

Chapter 8: In a nutshell, the story of Tiresias goes like this: Struck blind by Hera and given the gift of divination in return by Zeus, Tiresias is prophet and poet, a soothsayer whose visions are death and decay, warnings about the dangers of power and mighty aspiration. Literature's oracle, Tiresias persists through ancient myth to modern critique, wandering caves, barren deserts, and the circles of hell, seeing, despite his blindness, signs in the dark, in the smoke of burnt offerings, hearing fate in the songs of birds, their sharp whistles foreboding.

In death, deep in the underworld, Tiresias predicts man's fascination with strength and progress, and cautions Odysseus and his men not to eat the cattle of Helios, though their quest for achievement in the face of nature and the gods thrusts this warning aside. The men eat the cattle and are punished by death, Odysseus punished by the delay of his arduous journey home.

As man and Greece strengthen, Tiresias advises against the desire for unsanctioned knowledge in *Oedipus Rex*, for truth will destroy Oedipus, threaten prosperous Thebes. Eager for the forbidden, Oedipus ignores the warning and discovers he has murdered his father the king, grieved and bedded his mother, betrayed his people. Seeking redemption, Oedipus gouges his eyes and wanders in darkness, isolated and lamenting as Thebes is left plagued by tragedy.

Centuries later the prophecies persist—ignored. At the height of the Renaissance, perhaps the ultimate testament to man's achievement, Tiresias is punished in *The Divine Comedy*'s fourth pit of hell, his head twisted backward to prevent him from divining impending destruction. Tiresias condemned and his visions suppressed, Dante continues his journey toward enlightenment.

In Tennyson's *Tiresias*, man's mounting anger fuels his progress, reaping physical catastrophe—earthquakes, darkness, famine, plague. Entire cities go mad, tyranny rules and corrupts, power and desire go uncontrolled. Fate shadows even human prayer. And baleful birds spiral continuously, diving down to scavenge what remains.

Eliot's *The Waste Land* is the near completion of the vision in the smoke, the birdsong admonition. Realities, fragmented and disjointed, are broken, barren beyond hope. Tiresias is mournful narrator, observer of a world of insanity and infertility, deception and degradation. Pervading the landscape is an unrelenting ache for the past. The result of progress and pride, man is sentenced to a desolate home, hollow with death, filthy with decay—the blind seeing for centuries the apocalypse to come. —(courtesy of Sarah Fawn Montgomery)

Chapter 12: The original *Incredible Hulk* TV series also spawned several "remakes" and "revisitations" to the original story of the Incredible Hulk, which was first told in Marvel Comics. TV remake titles include *The Death of the Incredible Hulk* (1990, TV; a.k.a. *The Death of the Incredible Hulk: The Movie* [video box title]), *The Incredible Hulk Returns* (1988, TV), *The Trial of the Incredible Hulk* (1989, TV), *The Incredible Hulk: Death in the Family* (1977, TV; a.k.a. *The Return of the Incredible Hulk)*, and *The Incredible Hulk: Married* (1978, TV; a.k.a. *Bride of the Incredible Hulk)*. The TV show's closing song, titled "Superheroes," was originally written for *The Rocky Horror Picture Show*. (Information from imdb.com.)

Book 3: Fallout

Chapter 2: Though some later reports suggest there may have been more deaths than originally reported during the 2006 heat wave, estimates are that at least 141 people died in California and 22 in Fresno alone.

Chapter 8: John Milius is currently remaking *Red Dawn*, and it is supposedly scheduled for a 2010 release. The new adaptation is rumored to feature not Russian, Cuban, or Nicaraguan invaders, but legions of Red Chinese, and it is set not in the arid Rocky Mountain West but in the moist and lush Pacific Northwest.

Chapter 10: The quote referring to Reagan's reaction to the movie is taken from the epic presidential biography *Dutch*, by Edmund Morris. The quote from Meyer, identified as being from another interview, is from one with John Niccum of *The Lawrence Journal-World*, from November 19, 2003.

Book 4: The Returning End

The quote from George W. Bush was taken from MSNBC at www.msnbc.msn.com/id/18573872/.

The day after the storm, FEMA agents swooped in and moved quickly through town, gathering all the guns they could dig up. They entered my aunt's basement, found their way to a back room, pried open a locked cabinet, and removed several shotguns and rifles that belonged to my uncle and, before that, my grandfather. They made no effort to catalog the locations where guns were found or removed and simply piled all of them into a tractor-trailer. They then required the citizens of Greensburg to produce serial numbers and licenses in order to claim their guns.

Chapter 5: What follows is a partial list of other signs found in Greensburg on June 15 and 16, 2007.

- ANTIQUES FOR SALE: Sign propped up in front of a pile of bricks that used to be an old church turned antique store.
- LIQUOR LOUNGE: Sign for the first business to reopen in Greensburg after the storm, one of the first and only signs of life visible as you come into town on Highway 54.
- MAID WANTED: Spray-painted on the side of a house that had been knocked off its foundation, most of its windows blown out, and had large portions of the roof missing.
- THERE'S NO PLACE LIKE HOME: Spray-painted on the siding of a house that had been picked up and dropped. The words were written above a pair of ruby red slippers, fake legs, and striped stockings that had been carefully wedged under the house.
- PLEASE KEEP OUT and YES, YOU: My dad spray-painted these words in orange on the front of my Aunt Judy's house and on a large wing-back chair he used to block the front door. People had been coming into her house and climbing up to what was left of the third floor to stand and look at the destruction. They found boot prints in the dust and cigarette butts in the rubble. Looters had come too. And maybe they'd been in her house as well. Nobody was sure. Soon, the National Guard would patrol the streets in jeeps and big trucks.

❋ F, V, and X: These letters, or some combination of them, had been spray-painted on most of the remaining houses in Greensburg. It wasn't clear to anyone I asked what the letters meant, but speculation was that X indicated that the house had been checked by search and rescue, the F showed that the resident had been found, and the V meant that the house was vacant.

❋ And more signs: JD's BBQ WILL RETURN, GO AWAY, KEEP OUT, THANK YOU, RELIEF WORKERS, YOUR BABY'S FACE—this last one inexplicably spray-painted on the siding of a yellow house below a black-and-white spray-painted picture of Jesus with a crown of thorns. The house sat on the corner of Bay and Highway 54, three houses down from my Aunt Judy's house. It was visible to anyone who passed through, one of the last things visible before driving out of town.

Appendix 3
General Author Notes and Acknowledgments

Publication Credits:

The chapter "The Mutants Shall Inherit" was published first as "Wolf-Ants of the High Plains" in the online magazine *Freshyarn.com*. Other sections from the book were published first as "After the Day After" in *The Ruminator*, "Anticipating the Storm" and "After the Storm", in *Colorado Review*, and "Cornflake Fallout" in *New South*.

Photographs:

Source for photograph of *Tragic Prelude*, Book 1: Defense Visual Information Center Still HDSN9901774. Date Shot: 1 Jan 1937. Author: John Steuart Curry, for the Creator, Department of the Interior. National Park Service. Civil War Centennial Commission.

Permission: This work is in the public domain in the United States because it is a work of the United States Federal Government under the terms of Title 17, Chapter 1, Section 105 of the US Code. See Copyright.

Source for images, Book 2 and Book 3: Archive collection of *The Lawrence Journal-World*.

Permission: Grateful acknowledgement is made to the Kenneth W. Spencer Research Library at the University of Kansas for permission to reprint the images preceding Book 2 and Book 3.

Source for images, Book 4: Permission to reprint granted by the author.

Research and Writing:

I want to thank David Longhurst, Nathan Berg, Nicholas Meyer, and my parents for thoughtfully answering my questions about *The Day After* and other things. I also want to thank anyone who has shared their *Day After* story with me over the years (there are many of you) and I invite you to visit the site (myatomicangst.blogspot.com) to share your own story of *The Day After* or of growing up in the apocalyptic '80s.

This book could not have taken the form it has without the patient, guiding, and necessarily critical hand of Luke Gerwe, editor extraordinaire. I was happy to have him as a trusted collaborator in the process. I also want to thank Anne Horowitz and Denise Oswald and the other folks with Soft Skull Press for believing in the project, and the folks at Counterpoint for believing in Soft Skull. The book also could not have been written without the less-than-patient, frantic, angst-ridden, urgent influence of Metallica's first two albums (*Kill 'Em All* and *Ride the Lightning*) played at high volume. And coffee. Lots and lots of coffee. As far as creative process goes, it was less a meditation than it was a mosh-pit brawl. I want to especially thank Sarah Fawn Montgomery for wading into the mosh pit (so to speak) with her elbows swinging and helping me do vitally important research and for providing insightful perspective and feedback on the manuscript. She is largely responsible for much of the material presented in the notes section. Many thanks also to David Hann for his assistance in procuring images for the book.

I wish to acknowledge the influence and inspiration of my students in the MFA programs at California State University, Fresno, and the University of New Orleans, and to recognize the support and encouragement for this project from Steve Almond, Sophie Beck, Tom Bissell, Adam Braver, Alex Espinoza, Connie Hales, John Hales, Kristen Iversen, Matt Roberts, David Shields, Steve Yarbrough, and many other excellent writers who I am lucky enough to have as friends and colleagues. Most of all, I want to thank my wife Rachel and my children for their love, tolerance, humor, and vitality.

Printed in the United States
by Baker & Taylor Publisher Services